Spelling, Writing, & Vocabulary K

Book One

Guyla Nelson

and

Saundra Scovell Lamgo

MILE-HI
PUBLISHERS ™

American Language Series and the
Mile-Hi Publishers logo are trademarks of
Mile-Hi Publishers,
a division of
MH Publishers, LLC

Distributed under license by
Lighthouse Publishers, LLC
PO Box 570
Greer, SC 29652
www.lighthousepublishers.com

ISBN-13 978-1-934470-02-2
ISBN-10 1-934470-02-3

Printed in China

① Read the letters of the alphabet together with your teacher.

a b c d e f g h i j k l m

n o p q r s t u v w x y z

② Notice how the letter **t** is formed.
Practice tracing and writing the letter **t**.

③ Trace and write the first letter for each picture.

   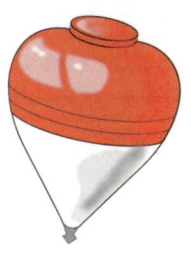   

④ Practice tracing and writing the letters.

| to | | | | | |

| ti | | | | | |

| ta | | | | | |

| co | | | | | |

| ca | | | | | |

⑤ Practice tracing and writing the words and phrases.

| tot | | a tot | |

| cot | | a cot | |

| dot | | a dot | |

| cat | | at a cat |

| it | |

| at | |

1 Read the letters of the alphabet together with your teacher.

a b c d e f g h i j k l m

n o p q r s t u v w x y z

2 Notice how the letter **e** is formed.
Practice tracing and writing the letter **e**.

e	e	e

e	e	e	e	e	e

e	e	e			

3 Trace and write the first letter for each picture.

  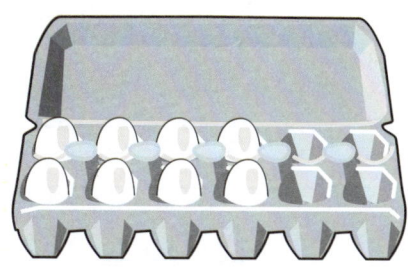

e	

e	

e	

4 Practice tracing and writing the letters.

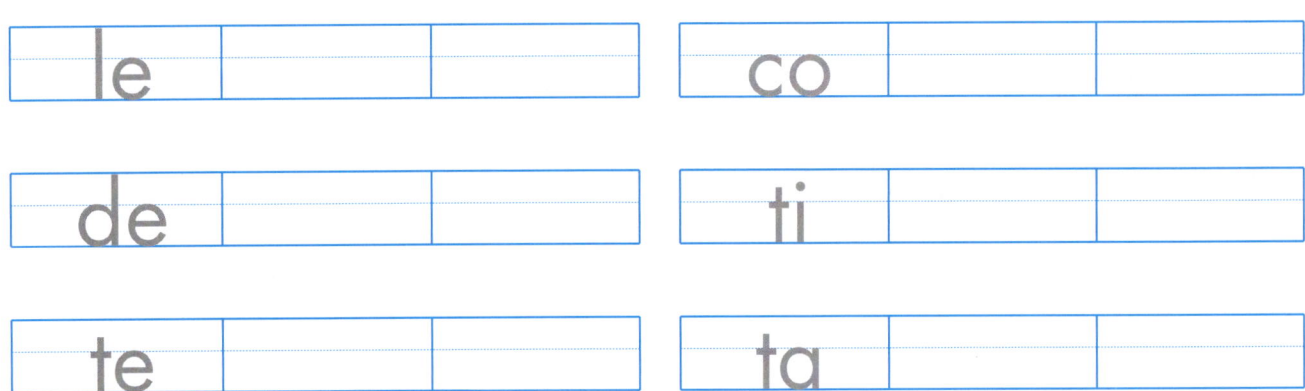

| le | | |

| co | | |

| de | | |

| ti | | |

| te | | |

| ta | | |

5 Practice tracing and writing the words and phrases.

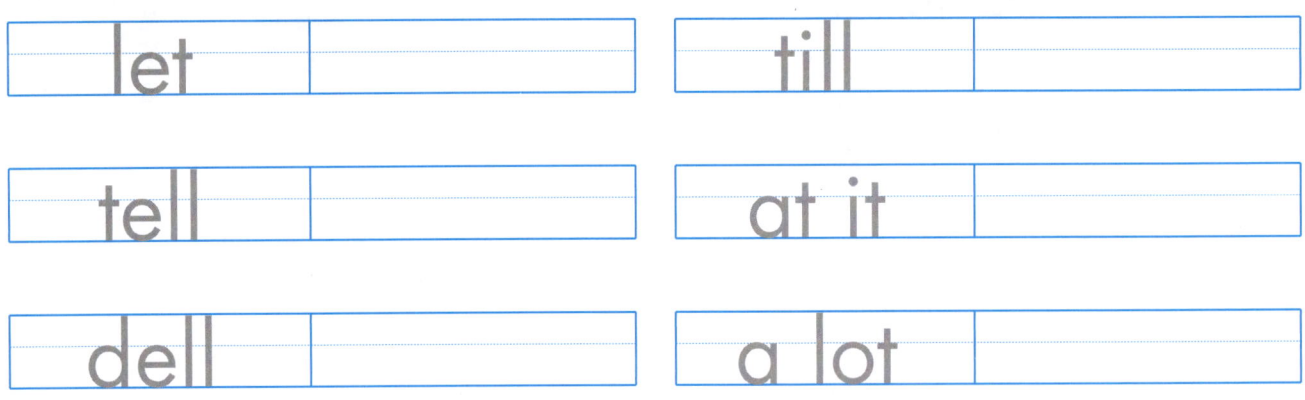

| let | |

| till | |

| tell | |

| at it | |

| dell | |

| a lot | |

6 Trace and write the phrases. Then draw a line from the phrase to the correct picture.

| a cat | |

| a cot | |

1 Read the letters of the alphabet together with your teacher.

a b c d e f g h i j k l m

n o p q r s t u v w x y z

2 Notice how the letter **f** is formed.
Practice tracing and writing the letter **f**.

f f f

f f f f f f f

f f f

3 Trace and write the first letter for each picture.

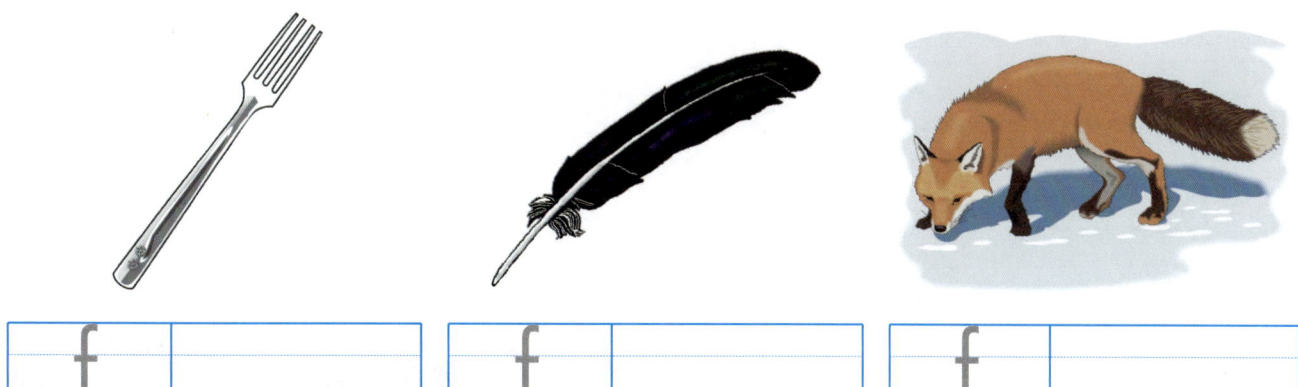

f f f

4 Practice tracing and writing the letters.

| fo | | | | fe | | |

| fi | | | | le | | |

| fa | | | | te | | |

5 Practice tracing and writing the words.

| fill | | | fat | |

| fell | | | fit | |

| fad | | | fed | |

6 Trace and write the words.

| off | | | doff | |

| if | |

7 Read the sentence.

Dad fed a fat cat.

1 Read the letters of the alphabet together with your teacher.

a b c d e f g h i j k l m

n o p q r s t u v w x y z

2 Notice how the letter **u** is formed.
Practice tracing and writing the letter **u**.

u   u   u

u   u   u   u   u   u

u   u   u

3 Trace and write the first letter for each picture.

u   u   u

4 Practice tracing and writing the letters.

| lu | | |

| tu | | |

| du | | |

| fu | | |

| cu | |

5 Practice tracing and writing the words.

| cull | |

| cud | |

| lull | |

| dud | |

| dull | |

| cut | |

6 Color the umbrella.

1 Read the letters of the alphabet together with your teacher.

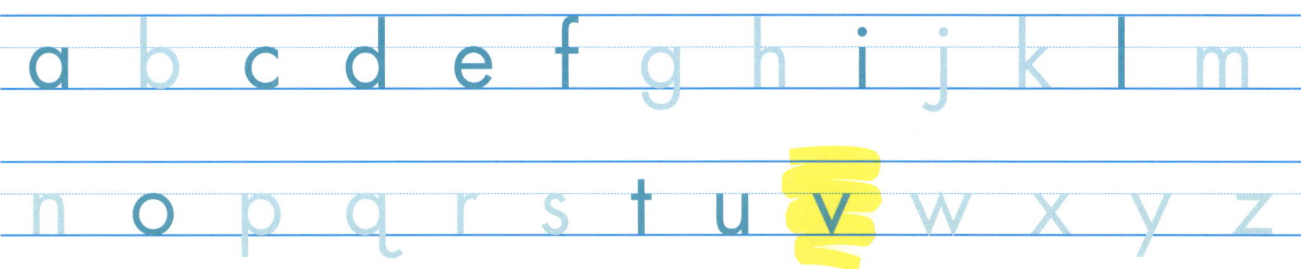

a b c d e f g h i j k l m

n o p q r s t u v w x y z

2 Notice how the letter **v** is formed.
Practice tracing and writing the letter **v**.

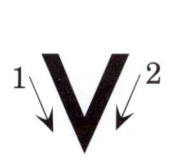 

3 Trace and write the first letter for each picture.

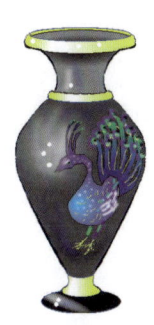  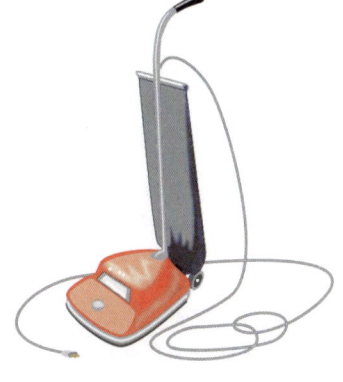

4 Practice tracing and writing the letters.

| vo | | | | lu | | |

| vi | | | | du | | |

| va | | | | cu | | |

| ve | | | | tu | | |

| vu | | | | fu | | |

5 Practice tracing and writing the words and the phrase.

| vat | | | cut | |

| vet | | | of | |

| a vet | | | dull | |

1 Read the letters of the alphabet together with your teacher.

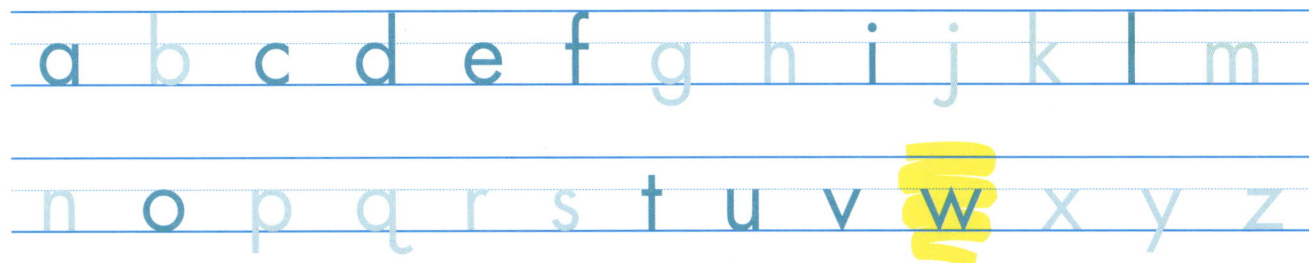

a b c d e f g h i j k l m

n o p q r s t u v w x y z

2 Notice how the letter **w** is formed.
Practice tracing and writing the letter **w**.

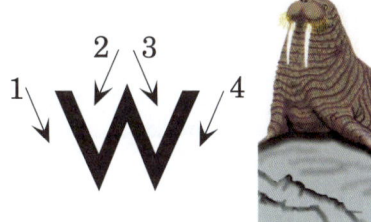

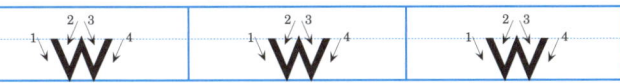

| w | w | w | w | w | w |

| w | w | w | | | |

3 Trace and write the first letter for each picture.

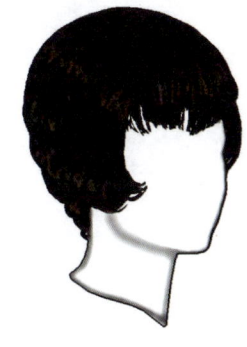  

| w | | | w | | | w | |

Practice tracing and writing the letters.

wi			vo		

wa			fi		

we			ca		

va			te		

ve			du		

5 Practice tracing and writing the words and the phrase.

well		wit	

will		wed	

a well	

1 Read the letters of the alphabet together with your teacher.

a b c d e f g h i j k l m

n o p q r s t u v w x y z

2 Notice how the letter **s** is formed.
Practice tracing and writing the letter **s**.

s s s

s s s s s s

s s s

3 Trace and write the first letter for each picture.

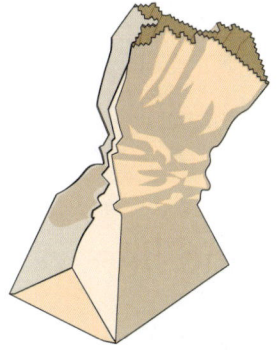
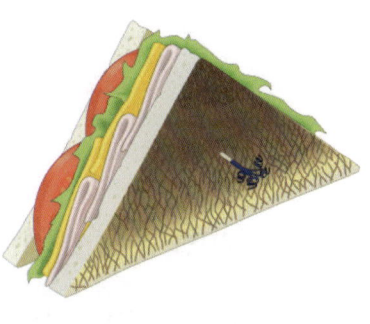

s
s
s

4 Practice tracing and writing the letters and words.

so				loss	
si				less	
sa				sass	
se				toss	
su				fuss	

5 Trace and write the words.

| sod | | cod | | sad | |

| sill | | lass | |

6 Write the sentence on the line.
A lad will fuss at a lass.

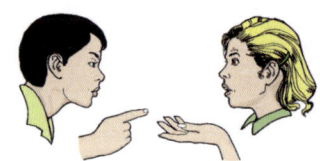

1 Read the letters of the alphabet together with your teacher.

a b c d e f g h i j k l m

n o p q r s t u v w x y z

2 Notice how the letter **h** is formed.
Practice tracing and writing the letter **h**.

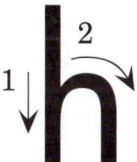 

h h h

h h h h h h

h h h

3 Trace and write the first letter for each picture.

  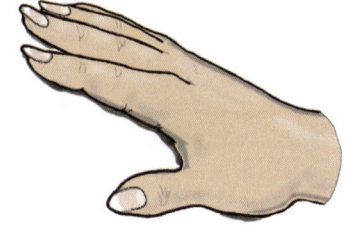

h h h

4 Practice tracing and writing the letters and words.

ho			hot	
hi			hit	
ha			had	
he			hid	
hu			hull	

5 Practice tracing and writing the words.

hat		hit	
hats		hits	
hut		sit	
huts		sits	
huff		doff	
huffs		doffs	

1 Read the letters of the alphabet together with your teacher.

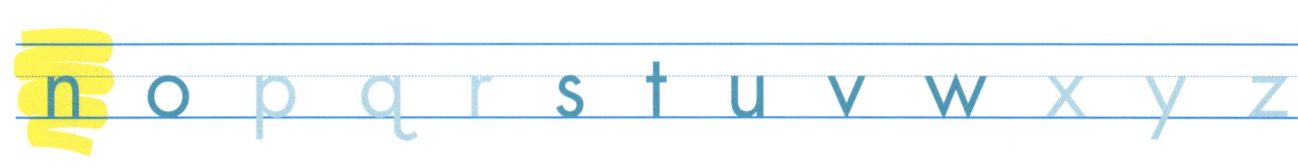

a b c d e f g h i j k l m

n o p q r s t u v w x y z

2 Notice how the letter **n** is formed.
Practice tracing and writing the letter **n**.

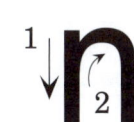 

n   n   n

n   n   n   n   n   n

n   n   n

3 Trace and write the words.

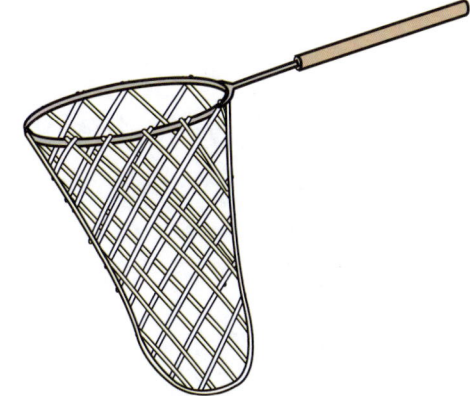

nut

net

4 Practice tracing and writing the letters and words.

| no | | | | as | | |

| ni | | | | has | | |

| na | | | | is | | |

| ne | | | | his | | |

| nu | | | | was | | |

5 Practice tracing and writing the words.

| hill | | |

| not | | | hiss | | |

| nod | | | tan | | |

6 Trace and write the word under the picture.

| can | | | fan | | | van | |

Name

1 Read the letters of the alphabet together with your teacher.

a b c d e f g h i j k l m

n o p q r s t u v w x y z

2 Notice how the letter **r** is formed.
Practice tracing and writing the letter **r**.

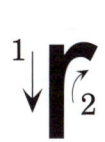

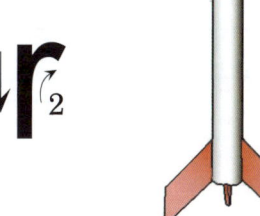

r r r

r   r   r   r   r   r

r   r   r

3 Trace and write the words.

rat

rod

4 Practice tracing and writing the letters and words.

ro		

nods	

ri		

lids	

ra		

lads	

re		

weds	

ru		

suds	

5 Trace and write the words under the pictures.

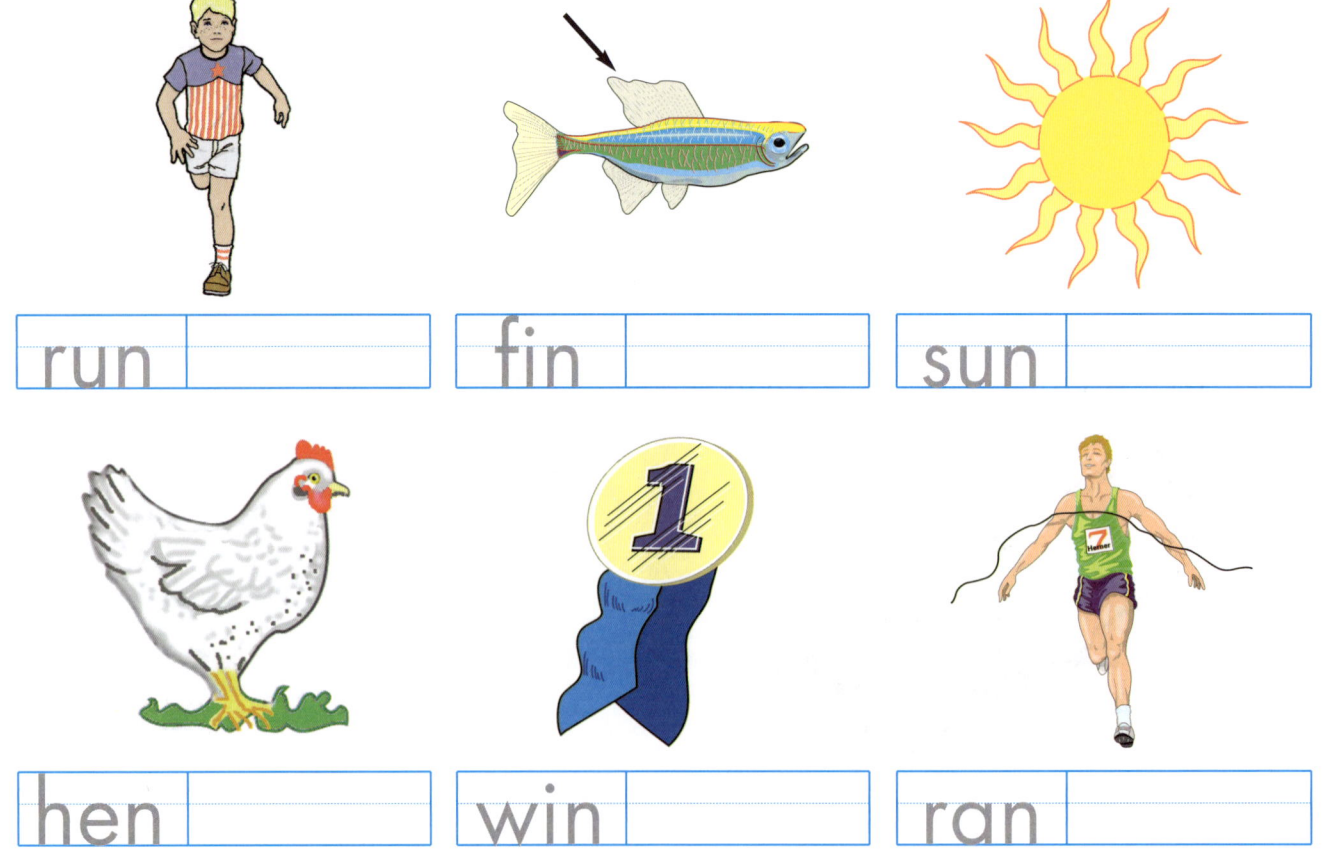

run	

fin	

sun	

hen	

win	

ran	

Name _____

1 Read the letters of the alphabet together with your teacher.

a b c d e f g h i j k l m

n o p q r s t u v w x y z

2 Notice how the letter **m** is formed.
Practice tracing and writing the letter **m**.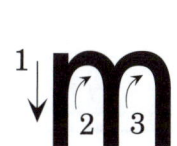

m m m

m m m m m m

m m m

3 Trace and write the words. Then draw a line to the correct picture.

| mat | |

| man | |

| mill | |

4 Practice tracing and writing the letters and words.

mo			moss		

mi			miss		

ma			mad		

me			mess		

mu			mud		

5 Practice tracing and writing the words and phrases.

ham		dam	

hum		dim	

him		sum	

a fat hen	

ten men on a hill

① Read the letters of the alphabet together with your teacher.

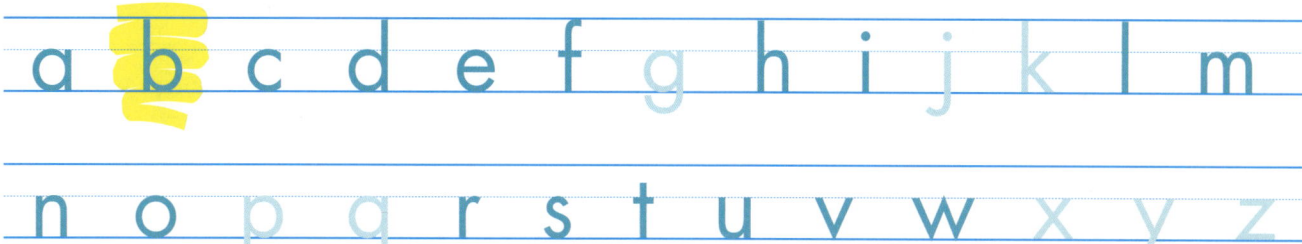

a b c d e f g h i j k l m

n o p q r s t u v w x y z

② Notice how the letter **b** is formed.
Practice tracing and writing the letter **b**.

b b b

b b b b b b

b b b

③ Trace and write the words.

bat   bun   bed

4 Practice tracing and writing the letters and words.

bo				dams	
bi				dims	
ba				hams	
be				hums	
bu				sums	

5 Read each word and then write it.

bet

but

bit

bin

bad

bid

bud

tab

web

rib

rob

rub

1 Read the letters of the alphabet together with your teacher.

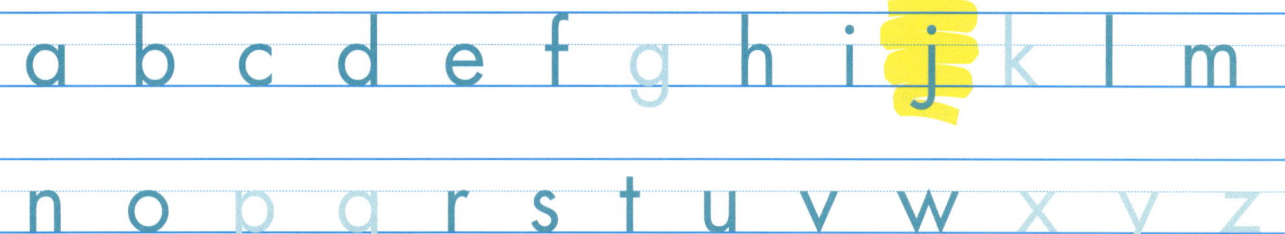

a b c d e f g h i j k l m

n o p q r s t u v w x y z

2 Notice how the letter **j** is formed.
Practice tracing and writing the letter **j**.

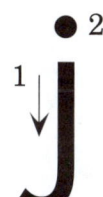

j j j

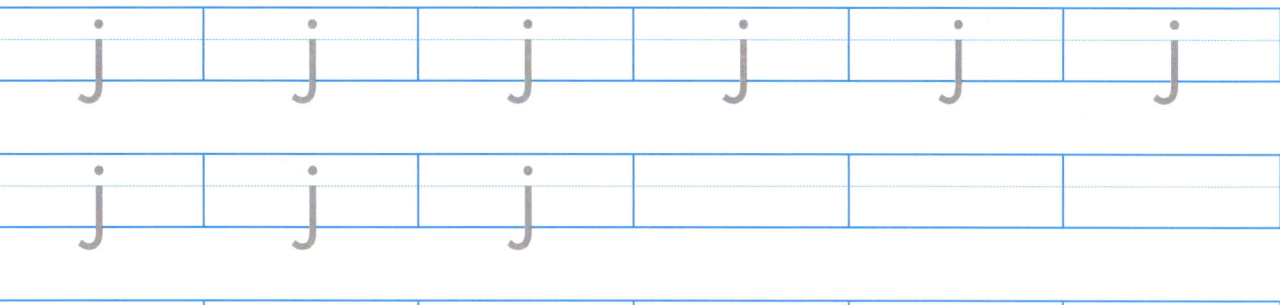

j j j j j j

j j j

j

3 Trace and write the words. Then draw a line to the
correct picture.

jet

jam

jib

4 Practice tracing and writing the letters and words.

jo		

fobs	

ji		

fibs	

ja		

tabs	

je		

webs	

ju		

hubs	

5 Read each word and then write it.

jab _____   rim _____

job _____   ram _____

jut _____   cob _____

bell _____   cub _____

bill _____   tub _____

boss _____

Name

1 Read the letters of the alphabet together with your teacher.

a b c d e f g h i j k l m

n o p q r s t u v w x y z

2 Notice how the letter **x** is formed.
Practice tracing and writing the letter **x**.

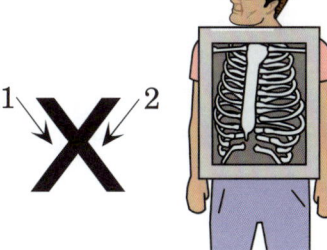

x   x   x

x   x   x   x   x   x

x   x   x

3 Trace and write the word under the picture.

box

6

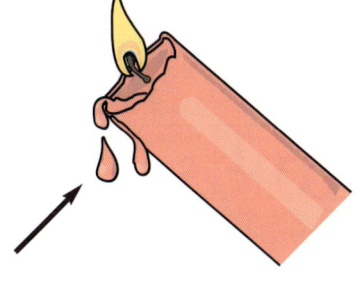

six   wax

4 Practice tracing and writing the letters and words.

ax			lax	

ex			vex	

ix			fix	

ox			fox	

mix			tax	

5 Practice tracing and writing the words.

dolls		lolls	

bells		tells	

bills		fills	

hills		sells	

mills		culls	

Name

1 Read the letters of the alphabet together with your teacher.

a b c d e f g h i j k l m

n o p q r s t u v w x y z

2 Notice how the letter **g** is formed.
Practice tracing and writing the letter **g**.

g¹↓² g¹↓² g¹↓²

g g g g g g

g g g

g

3 Trace and write the words.

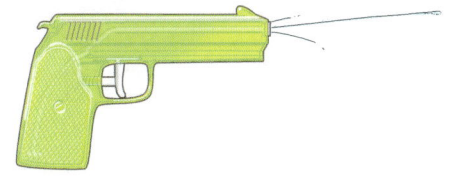

gum   gun   gull

4 Practice tracing and writing the letters.

| ga | | | | ag | | |

| go | | | | eg | | |

| gu | | | | ig | | |

| bo | | | | og | | |

| bu | | | | ug | | |

5 Read each word and then write it.

gab _____

gas _____

got _____

gut _____

bag _____

beg _____

leg _____

big _____

bog _____

hog _____

bug _____

jug _____

1 Read the letters of the alphabet together with your teacher.

a b c d e f g h i j k l m

n o p q r s t u v w x y z

2 Notice how the letter **y** is formed.
Practice tracing and writing the letter **y**.

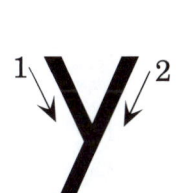 

y   y   y

y   y   y   y   y   y

y   y   y

y

3 Practice tracing and writing the letters.

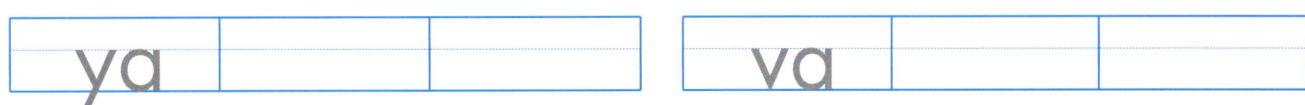

| ye | | | | ve | | |

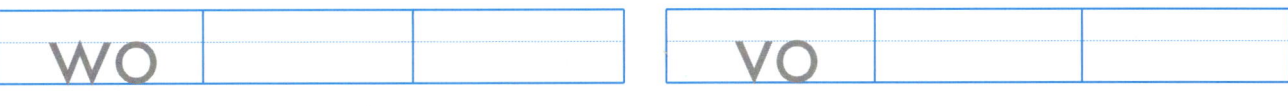

| ya | | | | va | | |

| wo | | | | vo | | |

| wi | | | | vi | | |

(4) Trace and write the words and then draw a line to the correct picture.

bag	
mug	
wig	
dog	
leg	

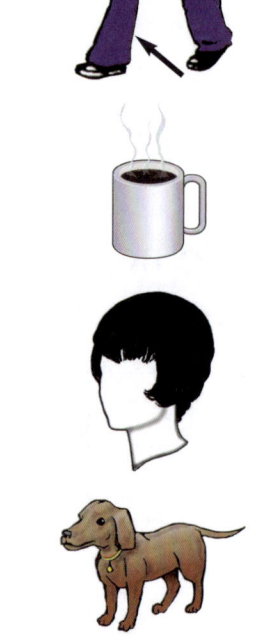

(5) Practice tracing and writing the words.

yell			hugs	
yam			jugs	
yet			rugs	
yes			rags	
bugs			logs	

① Read the letters of the alphabet together with your teacher.

a b c d e f g h i j k l m

n o p q r s t u v w x y z

② Notice how the letter **p** is formed.
Practice tracing and writing the letter **p**.

p   p   p

p   p   p   p   p   p

p   p   p

p

③ Trace and write the words.

pig   pan   pen

4 Practice tracing and writing the letters and words.

po			fans	
pi			cans	
pa			sins	
pe			wins	
pu			runs	

5 Read each word and then write it.

pad _____ pot _____

pod _____ pox _____

peg _____ pin _____

pat _____ pill _____

pet _____ pass _____

pit _____ puff _____

1 Read the letters of the alphabet together with your teacher.

a b c d e f g h i j k l m

n o p q r s t u v w x y z

2 Notice how the letter **q** is formed.
Practice tracing and writing the letter **q**.

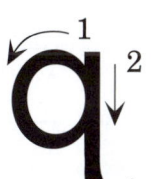 

q	q	q

q	q	q	q	q	q

q	q	q			

q					

3 Practice tracing and writing the letters. The letter **q** is always followed by the letter **u**.

qui		

que		

qua		

4 Practice tracing and writing the words.

quell		nips	

quit		naps	

quill		dips	

pep		lips	

cap		taps	

hip		yaps	

sap	

5 Trace and write the first two letters for each picture.

qu		qu		qu	

1 Read the letters of the alphabet together with your teacher.

a b c d e f g h i j k l m

n o p q r s t u v w x y z

2 Notice how the letter **k** is formed.
Practice tracing and writing the letter **k**.

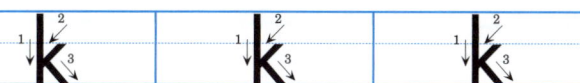

k   k   k   k   k   k

k   k   k

k

3 Read each word and then write it.

Rule 1

cab _____   tab _____

dab _____   fib _____

jab _____   bob _____

4   Read each word and then write it under the correct picture.

web   bib   rib   fob

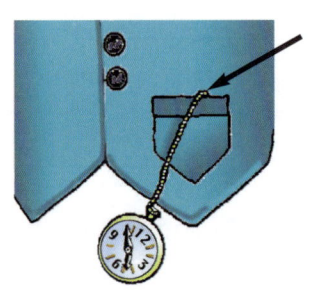  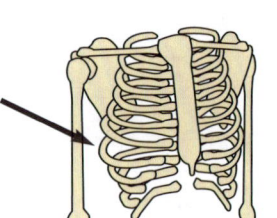 

_____ _____ _____ _____

5   Read each word and then write it.

Rule 1
<u>c</u>ob   _____

job   _____

mob   _____

rob   _____

sob   _____

Rule 1
<u>c</u>ub   _____

hub   _____

nub   _____

rub   _____

tub   _____

Review These Rules:

Rule 1:   **c** walks with **a**, **o**, or **u** to make the hard <u>c</u> sound.
Rule 13:   If a word has one vowel, the vowel is usually short.

1 Read the letters of the alphabet together with your teacher.

a b c d e f g h i j k l m

n o p q r s t u v w x y z

2 Notice how the letter **z** is formed.
Practice tracing and writing the letter **z**.

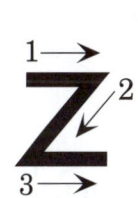

z z z z z z

z z z

z

3 Read each word and then write it under the correct picture.

Rule 5

bed   kid   bud

4 Read each word and then write it beside the correct picture.

Rule 1
lid   <u>c</u>od   lad   rod   mud

_____   _____

_____   _____

_____   _____

5 Read each word and then write it.

bad _____   fed _____

dad _____   led _____

had _____   red _____

mad _____   did _____

pad _____   hid _____

sad _____   nod _____

Review These Rules:

Rule 1:   **c** walks with **a**, **o**, or **u** to make the hard <u>c</u> sound.

Rule 5:   **k** walks with **e**, **i**, or **y** to make the **k** sound.

Rule 13:   If a word has one vowel, the vowel is usually short.

1 Notice how the capital letter **C** is formed. Practice tracing and writing the letters.

C C C

C   C   C   C   C   C   C

C

c

2 Read each word and then write it.

Rule 6
off

Rule 6
buff

Rule 6
huff

Rule 6
muff

Rule 6
puff

Rules 2, 21
gāg

Rule 21
jāg

Rule 21
lāg

Rule 21
nāg

Rule 21
sāg

Rule 21
tāg

Rule 21
beg

3 Read each word and then write it under the correct picture.

Rule 6   Rules 1, 6   Rule 21   Rule 21

doff   c̲uff   bag̅   rag̅

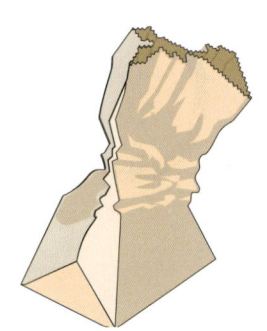  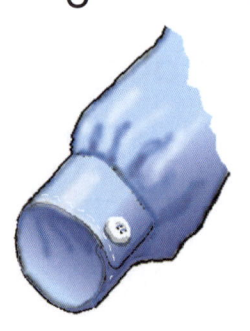 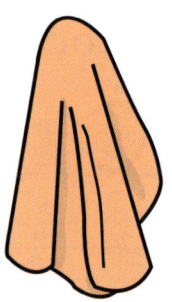

---

4 Draw a line from the word to the correct picture.

Rule 21
wag̅

 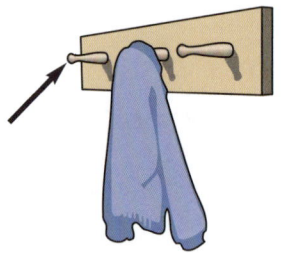

Rules 5, 21
keg̅

Rule 21
leg̅

Rule 21
peg̅

Review These Rules:

Rule 1:   **c** walks with **a**, **o**, or **u** to make the hard **c̲** sound.

Rule 2:   **g** walks with **a**, **o**, or **u** to make the hard **g̅** sound.

Rule 5:   **k** walks with **e**, **i**, or **y** to make the **k** sound.

Rule 6:   If a short-vowel word ends in **f**, **l**, **s**, or **z**, we usually double the final consonant.

Rule 13:   If a word has one vowel, the vowel is usually short.

Rule 21:   **g** has the hard **g̅** sound at the end of a word.

Name _____

Lesson 28

1 Notice how the capital letter **O** is formed.
Practice tracing and writing the letters.

O   O   O

O   O   O   O   O   O

O

O

2 Read each word and then write it under the correct picture.

Rule 21   Rule 21   Rule 21   Rule 21
piḡ   wiḡ   doḡ   loḡ

   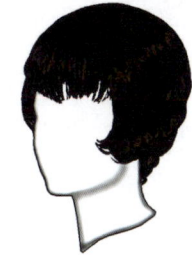

_____ _____ _____ _____

3 Read each word and then write it.

Rule 21
duḡ _____

Rule 21
luḡ _____

Rule 21
huḡ _____

Rule 21
tuḡ _____

© Mile-Hi Publishers. Do not reproduce.

Spelling, Writing, & Vocabulary K, Book One   55

④ Draw a line from the word to the correct picture.

Rule 21
bug̅

Rule 21
jug̅

Rule 21
mug̅

Rule 21
rug̅

⑤ Read each word and then write it.

Rule 21
big̅ _____

Rule 21
dig̅ _____

Rule 21
fig̅ _____

Rule 21
jig̅ _____

Rule 21
bog̅ _____

Rule 21
fog̅ _____

Rule 21
hog̅ _____

Rule 21
jog̅ _____

Review These Rules:

Rule 13:   If a word has one vowel, the vowel is usually short.
Rule 21:   **g** has the hard g̅ sound at the end of a word.

Name

1 Notice how the capital letter **S** is formed.
   Practice tracing and writing the letters.

S¹

S¹   S¹   S¹

S   S   S   S   S   S

S

S

2 Read each word and then write it beside the correct picture.

Rule 7   Rule 7   Rule 7   Rule 7   Rule 7   Rule 7
badge   hedge   ledge   wedge   fudge   judge

_____

_____

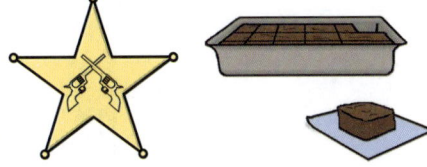
_____

_____

_____

3 Read each word and then write it.

Rule 7
edge _____

Rule 7
lodge _____

Rule 7
ridge _____

Rule 7
budge _____

Rule 7
dodge _____

Rule 7
nudge _____

4 Draw a line from the word to the correct picture.

Rule 6
bell

Rule 6
fell

Rule 6
well

Rule 6
yell

5 Read each word and then write it.

Rule 6
dell _____

Rule 6
sell _____

Rule 6
jell _____

Rule 6
tell _____

Review These Rules:

Rule 6: If a short-vowel word ends in **f**, **l**, **s**, or **z**, we usually double the final consonant.

Rule 7: In a short word, use **dge** if the **j** sound comes right after a short vowel.

Rule 13: If a word has one vowel, the vowel is usually short.

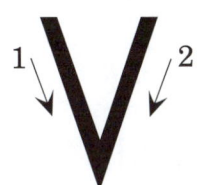

Lesson 30

① Notice how the capital letter **V** is formed. Practice tracing and writing the letters.

② Read each word and then write it under the correct picture.

Rule 6   Rule 6   Rule 6   Rule 6
bill   **hill**   **mill**   **pill**

   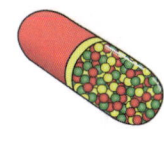   

③ Read each word and then write it.

Rule 6
dill

Rule 6
fill

Rule 6
ill

Rules 5, 6
kill

4 Draw a line from the word to the correct picture.

Rule 6
sill

Rule 6
doll

Rule 6
loll

Rules 2, 6
ḡull

5 Read each word and then write it.

Rule 6
rill _____

Rule 6
till _____

Rule 6
will _____

Rules 1, 6
c̲ull _____

Rule 6
dull _____

Rule 6
hull _____

Rule 6
lull _____

Rule 6
mull _____

Review These Rules:

Rule 1: **c** walks with **a**, **o**, or **u** to make the hard **c̲** sound.

Rule 2: **g** walks with **a**, **o**, or **u** to make the hard **ḡ** sound.

Rule 5: **k** walks with **e**, **i**, or **y** to make the **k** sound.

Rule 6: If a short-vowel word ends in **f**, **l**, **s**, or **z**, we usually double the final consonant.

Rule 13: If a word has one vowel, the vowel is usually short.

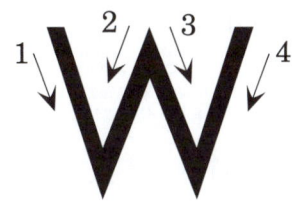

1 Notice how the capital letter **W** is formed. Practice tracing and writing the letters.

W W W W W W

W

W

2 Read each word and then write it beside the correct picture.

dam   ham   jam   ram   tam   yam

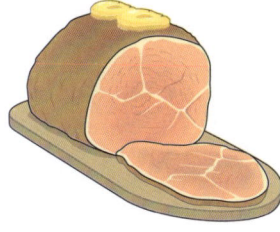

3 Read each word and then write it.

am		him	
bam		mom	
hem		bum	
dim		hum	

4 Draw a line from the word to the correct picture.

Rule 4
ġem

rim

$I + I = 2$

Rule 2
ḡum

mum

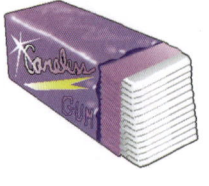

sum

Review These Rules:
Rule 2: g walks with **a**, **o**, or **u** to make the hard **ḡ** sound.
Rule 4: g walks with **e**, **i**, or **y** to make the soft **ġ** sound.
Rule 13: If a word has one vowel, the vowel is usually short.

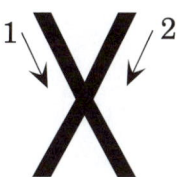

Lesson 32

1 Notice how the capital letter **X** is formed. Practice tracing and writing the letters.

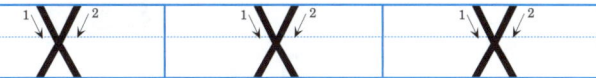

2 Read each word and then write it under the correct picture.

Rule 1

<u>c</u>an   fan   man   pan

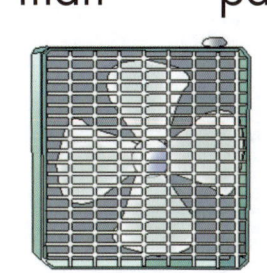

3 Read each word and then write it.

an   _____   tan   _____

ran   _____   van   _____

4 Draw a line from the word to the correct picture.

ten

bun

Rule 2
g̅un

sun

5 Read each word and then write it.

den _____

hen _____

men _____

pen _____

in _____

Rule 5
kin _____

sin _____

win _____

on _____

fun _____

run _____

Review These Rules:

Rule 1: **c** walks with **a**, **o**, or **u** to make the hard **c̲** sound.

Rule 2: **g** walks with **a**, **o**, or **u** to make the hard **g̅** sound.

Rule 5: **k** walks with **e**, **i**, or **y** to make the **k** sound.

Rule 13: If a word has one vowel, the vowel is usually short.

1 Notice how the capital letter **Z** is formed. Practice tracing and writing the letters.

2 Read each word and then write it.

Rule 2

g̅ap

lap

nap

sap

yap

pep

3 Read each word and then write it under the correct picture.

Rule 1

c̲ap   map   tap   hip

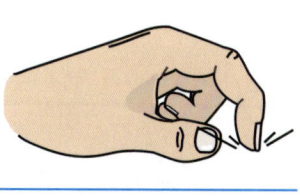

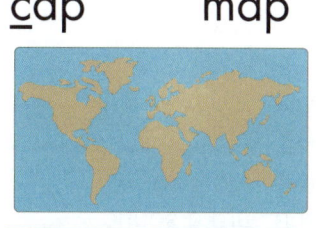

④ Read each word and then write it.

dip _____   tip _____

nip _____   zip _____

sip _____   up _____

⑤ Read each word and then write it under the correct picture.

lip   rip   hop   mop

pop   top   Rule 1 <u>c</u>up   pup

Name

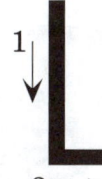

Lesson 34

1 Notice how the capital letter **L** is formed. Practice tracing and writing the letters.

2 Read each word and then write it under the correct picture.

Rule 6 bass Rule 6 lass Rule 6 pass

3 Read each word and then write it.

Rule 6 mass

Rule 6 less

Rule 6 sass

Rule 6 hiss

© Mile-Hi Publishers. Do not reproduce.

Spelling, Writing, & Vocabulary K, Book One 67

4 Read each word and then write it under the correct picture.

Rule 6   Rule 6   Rules 5, 6   Rule 6
miss   mess   kiss   toss

_____ _____ _____ _____
- - - - - - -   - - - - - - -   - - - - - - -   - - - - - - -
_____ _____ _____ _____

5 Read each word and then write it.

Rule 6   Rule 6
fuss   boss

Rule 6   Rule 6
muss   loss

                                          Rule 6
                                          moss

Review These Rules:

Rule 5:   **k** walks with **e**, **i**, or **y** to make the **k** sound.

Rule 6:   If a short-vowel word ends in **f**, **l**, **s**, or **z**, we usually double the final consonant.

Rule 13: If a word has one vowel, the vowel is usually short.

1 Notice how the capital letter **A** is formed. Practice tracing and writing the letters.

A A A

A A A A A A

A

a

2 Read each word and then write it under the correct picture.

Rule 1

bat c̲at hat mat

_____ _____ _____ _____

3 Read each word and then write it.

at _____   pat _____

fat _____   sat _____

4 Read each word and then write it under the correct picture.

rat   vat   jet   net

5 Read each word and then write it.

bet   _____   set   _____

let   _____   wet   _____

met   _____   yet   _____

6 Write each word to match its picture.

pet   vet

Review These Rules:

Rule 1:   c walks with **a**, **o**, or **u** to make the hard <u>c</u> sound.
Rule 13: If a word has one vowel, the vowel is usually short.

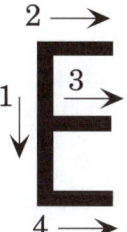

1 Notice how the capital letter **E** is formed. Practice tracing and writing the letters.

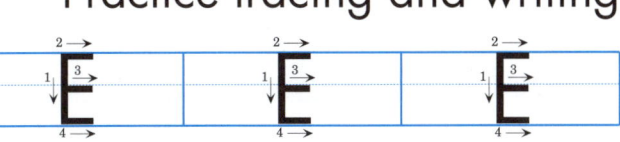

E   E   E   E   E   E

E

e

2 Read each word and then write it.

bit _____

fit _____

it _____

lit _____

sit _____

dot _____

3 Read each word and then write it under the correct picture.

Rule 5

hit   kit   pit   lot

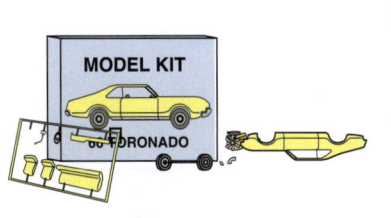

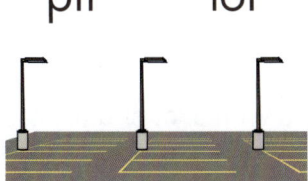

_____   _____   _____   _____

4 Read each word and then write it.

Rule 2

ḡot _____

jot _____

rot _____

not _____

but _____

rut _____

5 Read each word and then write it beside the correct picture.

Rule 1

hot   pot   tot   c̲ut   hut   nut

_____

_____

Review These Rules:

Rule 1:   c walks with **a**, **o**, or **u** to make the hard c̲ sound.

Rule 2:   g walks with **a**, **o**, or **u** to make the hard ḡ sound.

Rule 5:   k walks with **e**, **i**, or **y** to make the k sound.

Rule 13: If a word has one vowel, the vowel is usually short.

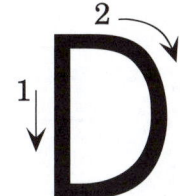
1 Notice how the capital letter **D** is formed. Practice tracing and writing the letters.

D D D

D D D D D D

D

d

2 Draw a line from the word to the correct picture.

6

Rule 27

ax

Rule 27

wax

Rule 27

mix

Rule 27

six

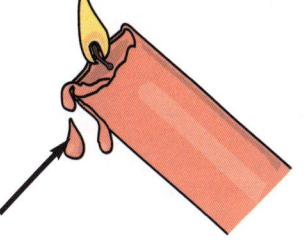

3 Read each word and then write it.

Rule 27
lax _____

Rule 27
tax _____

Rule 27
vex _____

Rule 27
fix _____

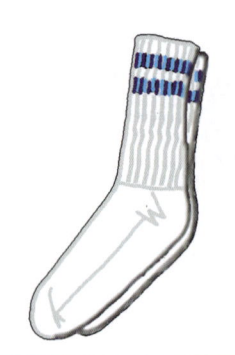

Rule 6
jazz _____

Rule 6
razz _____

Rule 6
fizz _____

Rule 6
buzz _____

Rule 6
fuzz _____

4 Read each word and then write it under the correct picture.

Rule 27   Rule 27   Rule 27   Rule 27
box   **fox**   **ox**   **sox**

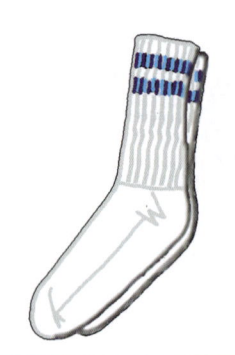

_____   _____   _____   _____

Review These Rules:

Rule 6:   If a short-vowel word ends in **f**, **l**, **s**, or **z**, we usually double the final consonant.

Rule 13: If a word has one vowel, the vowel is usually short.

Rule 27: Usually **x** at the end of a word has the soft **x** sound.

1 Notice how the capital letter **T** is formed. Practice tracing and writing the letters.

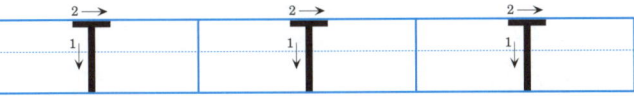

It Breaks the Rule!

2 These words break Rule 6. They do not end in a double consonant. Read each word and write it on the line.

	The soft **s** sound	The hard **s** sound
if	Rule 2	Rule 25
	ḡas	a**s**
*		Rule 25
o**f**	yes	ha**s**
		Rule 25
pal	sis	i**s**
		Rule 25
	bus	hi**s**
	us	

It Breaks the Rule!

3 The words below break Rule 6. They do not end in **f**, **l**, **s**, or **z**, but the final consonant is doubled. Circle the twin consonants at the end and then write the word.

add _____

odd _____

inn _____

Rule 21

eḡḡ _____

mitt _____

4 Read each sentence and circle the word that ends in twin consonants.

1. Did Dan nap at the inn?

2. Meg had an egg on a bun.

3. An odd bug lit on Jim.

4. Can Rex add the big sum?

5. Did the mitt fit Tim?

100
+ 200

Review These Rules:

Rule 2:   **g** walks with **a**, **o**, or **u** to make the hard **ḡ** sound.
Rule 6:   If a short-vowel word ends in **f**, **l**, **s**, or **z**, we usually double the final consonant.
Rule 13: If a word has one vowel, the vowel is usually short.
Rule 21: **g** has the hard **ḡ** sound at the end of a word.
Rule 25: Sometimes **s** has the hard **s̲** sound.
*Exception: In this word **f** has the hard **f̲** sound (like **v**).

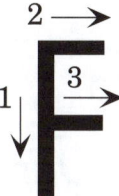

1. Notice how the capital letter **F** is formed. Practice tracing and writing the letters.

F F F

F F F F F F F

F

f

It Breaks the Rule!

2. These words break Rule 13 because they end in **e**, **o**, or **y**. Read each word below and listen to the long-vowel sound. Then write the word on the line.

bē _____   Rule 2   gō _____   bȳ _____

hē _____   hō _____   mȳ _____

mē _____   lō _____

wē _____   nō _____

yē _____   sō _____

(3) In these words **o** has the **o̤** sound. Read each word, write it on the line, and read the sentences.

Rule 17
do̤ _____

Rule 17
to̤ _____

1. Dan will tell Les to run.

2. A lad will not do his job.

It Breaks the Rule!

(4) These words break Rule 13 because the **ȯ** has the sound of short **ŭ**. Read each word and write it, pronouncing **ȯ** with a short **ŭ** sound. Then write the word on the line.

Rule 10
sȯn _____

Rule 10
tȯn _____

Rule 10
wȯn _____

2,000 lbs.

(5) Read each sentence. Circle each word where **ȯ** has the short **ŭ** sound.

1. Dan is not my son.

2. Will a ton of wax fill the van?

3. Jim won the badge.

Review These Rules:

Rule 2:   **g** walks with **a**, **o**, or **u** to make the hard **ḡ** sound.
Rule 10:   When **o** has the short **u** sound, it is marked **ȯ**.
Rule 13:   If a word has one vowel, the vowel is usually short.
Exception: If a short word with one vowel ends in **e**, **o**, or **y**, the vowel is usually long.
Rule 17:   When **o** has the sound of long **o̅o̅**, two dots are placed under the **o̤**.

Lesson 40

1 Notice how the capital letter **I** is formed. Practice tracing and writing the letters.

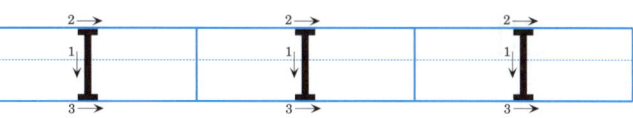

It Breaks the Rule!

2 In these words, **u̧** has the sound that we hear in the word **fu̧ll**. Read each word, write it, and read the sentences.

Rules 26, 6
bu̧ll _____

Put the bull in his pen.

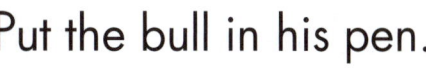

Rules 26, 6
fu̧ll _____

The jug is not full.

Rules 26, 6
pu̧ll _____

Pull the top off!

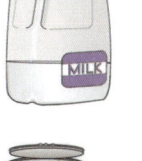

Rule 26
pu̧t _____

Put it by the rug.

It Breaks the Rule!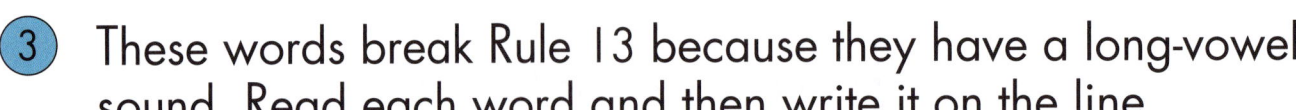

③ These words break Rule 13 because they have a long-vowel sound. Read each word and then write it on the line.

Rule 6
rōll _____

Rule 6
tōll _____

Read each sentence. Circle the long-vowel sound.

1. Did the bell toll?

2. Ned had jam on the roll.

It Breaks the Rule!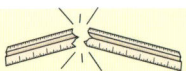

④ These words break Rule 13. After the **w** sound, the vowel **ạ** sometimes sounds like short **ŏ**. Read each word below and then write it. Listen to the **ạ** make the short **ŏ** sound.

Rule 28
wạd _____

Rules 28, 25
wạ̲s _____

Was a wad of gum on the ledge?

It Breaks the Rule!

⑤ This word breaks Rule 4. The hard **ḡ** sound is followed by **e**. Read the word and then write it.

ḡet _____

Review These Rules:

Rule 4: **g** walks with **e**, **i**, or **y** to make the soft **ġ** sound.

Rule 6: If a short-vowel word ends in **f**, **l**, **s**, or **z**, we usually double the final consonant.

Rule 13: If a word has one vowel, the vowel is usually short.

Rule 25: Sometimes **s** has the hard **s̲** sound.

Rule 26: When **u** has the sound of **u** as in **full**, one dot is placed under the **ụ**.

Rule 28: After **w**, **a** often has the short **ŏ** sound and is marked **ạ**.

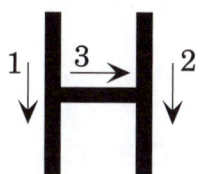

Lesson 41

1 Notice how the capital letter **H** is formed. Practice tracing and writing the letters.

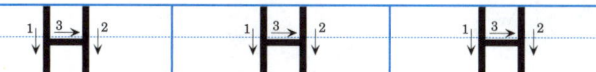

H H H H H H

H

h

2 Read each word and then write it under the correct picture.

Rule 6   Rule 6
chaff   chess   chin   chop

_____   _____   _____   _____

3 Read each word and then write it.

chap   _____   chat   _____

Rule 6   Rule 21
chill _____   chug   _____

chip   _____   chum   _____

4 Draw a line from the word to the correct picture.

Rule 39
ranch

Rule 39
bench

Rule 39
lunch

Rule 39
punch

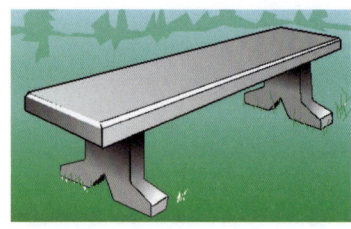

5 Read each word and then write it.

Rule 39
mulch
_____

Rule 39
bunch
_____

Rule 39
inch
_____

Rule 39
hunch
_____

Rule 39
pinch
_____

Rule 39
munch
_____

Review These Rules:

Rule 6: If a short-vowel word ends in **f**, **l**, **s**, or **z**, we usually double the final consonant.

Rule 13: If a word has one vowel, the vowel is usually short.

Rule 21: **g** has the hard **ḡ** sound at the end of a word.

Rule 39: If consonant **l**, **n**, or **r** comes between the vowel and the **ch** sound, it is spelled **ch**.

Name _____

1 Notice how the capital letter **N** is formed. Practice tracing and writing the letters.

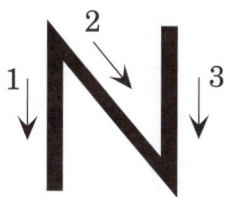

N N N

N N N N N N

N

n

2 Read each word and then write it under the correct picture.

Rule 38
hatch

Rule 38
latch

Rule 38
match

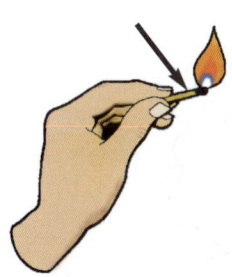

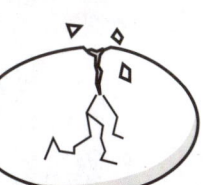

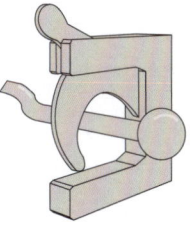

_____

_____

_____

Rule 38
ditch

Rule 38
hitch

Rule 38
hutch

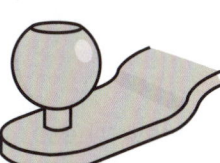

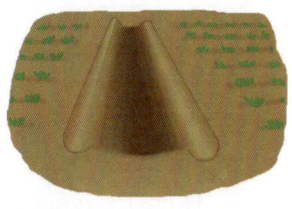

_____

_____

_____

3 Read each word and then write it.

Rule 38
batch _____

Rule 38
fetch _____

Rules 1, 38
<u>c</u>atch _____

Rule 38
itch _____

Rule 38
patch _____

Rule 38
pitch _____

Rule 38
etch _____

Rule 38
notch _____

Review These Rules:

Rule 1:   **c** walks with **a**, **o**, or **u** to make the hard <u>c</u> sound.
Rule 13:   If a word has one vowel, the vowel is usually short.
Rule 38:   In a short word, use **tch** if the **ch** sound comes right after a short vowel.

Name _____

1 Notice how the capital letter **R** is formed. Practice tracing and writing the letters.

R   R   R

R   R   R   R   R   R

R

r

2 Read each word and then write it.

Rule 21
shag _____   shod _____

Rule 6
shall _____   shot _____

sham _____   shun _____

shin _____   shut _____

3 Draw a line from the word to the correct picture.

shed

Rule 6
shell

ship

shop

4 Choose the correct word to finish each sentence and write it on the line.

shot / shut

1. Tim will _____ the pigs in the pen.

shall / shell

2. Can we _____ the nuts?

ship / shop

3. Sam will go on a big _____ .

Review These Rules:

Rule 6: If a short-vowel word ends in **f**, **l**, **s**, or **z**, we usually double the final consonant.

Rule 13: If a word has one vowel, the vowel is usually short.

Rule 21: **g** has the hard **ḡ** sound at the end of a word.

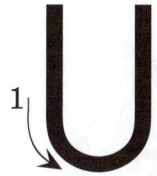

1 Notice how the capital letter **U** is formed. Practice tracing and writing the letters.

U U U

U U U U U U

U

u

2 Read each word and then write it.

ash _____

bash _____

Rule 1
c̲ash _____

dash _____

Rule 2
ḡash _____

hash _____

lash _____

rash _____

mesh _____

wish _____

Spelling, Writing, & Vocabulary K, Book One　87

3 Read each word and then write it under the correct picture.

mash   sash   dish   fish

_____ _____ _____ _____

4 Read each word and then write it.

Rule 2
ḡush _____   rush _____

hush _____

lush _____

mush _____

Review These Rules:

Rule 1: c walks with **a**, **o**, or **u** to make the hard <u>c</u> sound.
Rule 2: g walks with **a**, **o**, or **u** to make the hard ḡ sound.
Rule 13: If a word has one vowel, the vowel is usually short.

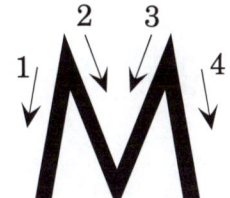

1 Notice how the capital letter **M** is formed. Practice tracing and writing the letters.

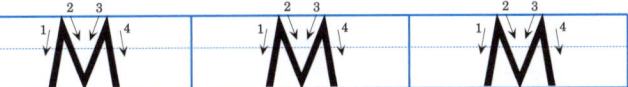

M M M M M M

M

m

2 Read each word, using the hard, voiced **th** sound, and then write it.

Rule 40
<u>th</u>an

Rule 40
<u>th</u>em

Rule 40
<u>th</u>at

Rule 40
<u>th</u>en

3 Practice tracing and writing this word that begins with the soft, voiceless **th** sound.

thin

thin

④ Read each word using the soft, voiceless **th** sound and then write it.

width _____   depth _____

fifth _____   sixth _____

length _____   with _____

tenth _____

⑤ Draw a line from the word to the correct picture.

bath

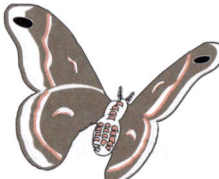

math

path

$1 + 1 = 2$

moth

Review These Rules:

Rule 13: If a word has one vowel, the vowel is usually short.
Rule 40: The voiced sound of **th** has a horizontal mark underneath <u>th</u>.

① Notice how the capital letter **B** is formed. Practice tracing and writing the letters.

B B B

B B B B B B

B

b

② Read each word and then write it.

Rule 37
wham _____

Rule 37
whip _____

Rule 37
when _____

Rules 37, 6
whizz _____

Rules 37, 6
whiff _____

Rule 37
whop _____

③ Trace and write the beginning sound for each picture.

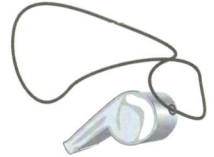

wh   wh   wh

4 Read each word and then write it under the correct picture.

Rule 5

fang   king   ring   wing

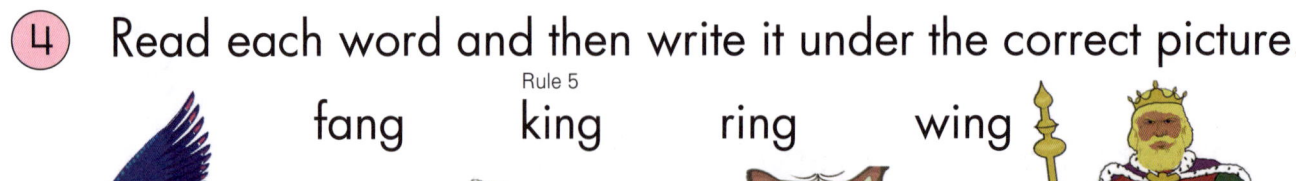

_____   _____   _____   _____

5 Read each word and then write it.

bang	_____	thing _____
Rule 2 gang	_____	dong _____
hang	_____	long _____
rang	_____	song _____
sang	_____	hung _____
ding	_____	rung _____
sing	_____	sung _____

Review These Rules:

Rule 2: **g** walks with **a**, **o**, or **u** to make the hard **ḡ** sound.

Rule 5: **k** walks with **e**, **i**, or **y** to make the **k** sound.

Rule 6: If a short-vowel word ends in **f**, **l**, **s**, or **z**, we usually double the final consonant.

Rule 13: If a word has one vowel, the vowel is usually short.

Rule 37: Sometimes when **w** and **h** go walking, they make the consonant-digraph sound — **wh**.

1 Notice how the capital letter **J** is formed.
Practice tracing and writing the letters.

J ↓1

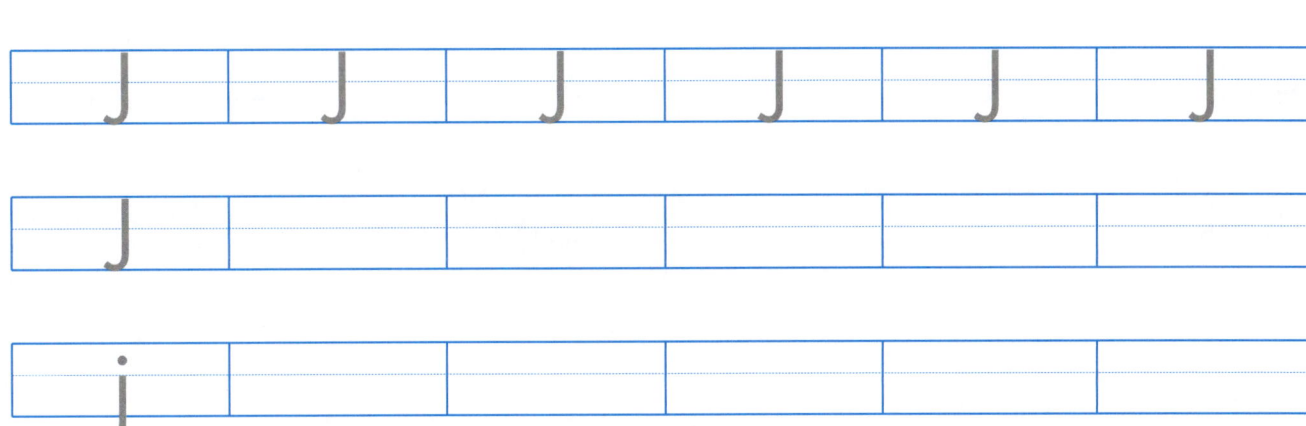

2 Read each word and then write it.

bank _____   thank _____

sank _____   yank _____

3 Read each word and then write it under the correct picture.

tank   link   mink

_____   _____   _____

Spelling, Writing, & Vocabulary K, Book One   93

4 **Read each word and then write it.**

ink _____

honk _____

Rule 5
kink _____

chunk _____

pink _____

junk _____

think _____

sunk _____

5 **Draw a line from the word to the correct picture.**

sink

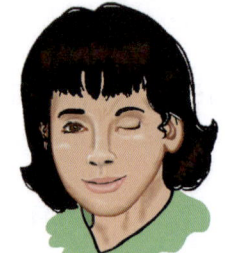

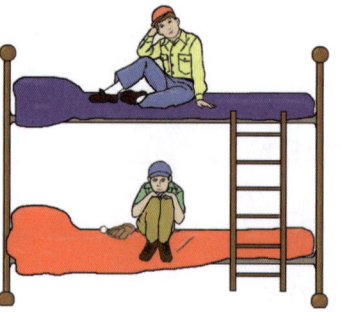

wink

bunk

Review These Rules:

Rule 5:   **k** walks with **e**, **i**, or **y** to make the **k** sound.

Rule 13:   If a word has one vowel, the vowel is usually short.

1 Notice how the capital letter **G** is formed.
   Practice tracing and writing the letters.

G¹←2 G¹←2 G¹←2 G¹←2

G G G G G G

G

g

2 Read each word and then write it.

blab _____

drab _____

grab _____

Rule 46

scab _____

slab _____

stab _____

3 Choose the correct word to finish each sentence and
   write it on the line.

drab / grab

1. Jim has on a _____ hat.

stab / slab

2. Do not _____ the bug!

4 Draw a line from the word to the correct picture.

crab

crib

club

5 Read each word and then write it.

blob _____

grub _____

snub _____

stub _____

Review These Rules:

Rule 13: If a word has one vowel, the vowel is usually short.
Rule 46: **sc** walks with **a**, **o**, or **u** to make the **sk** sound.

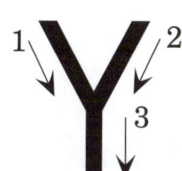
1 Notice how the capital letter **Y** is formed.
Practice tracing and writing the letters.

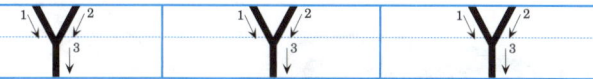

2 Read each word and then write it.

brad

clad

glad

bled

fled

3 Read each word and then write it under the correct picture.

Rule 47

sled   skid   clod   spud

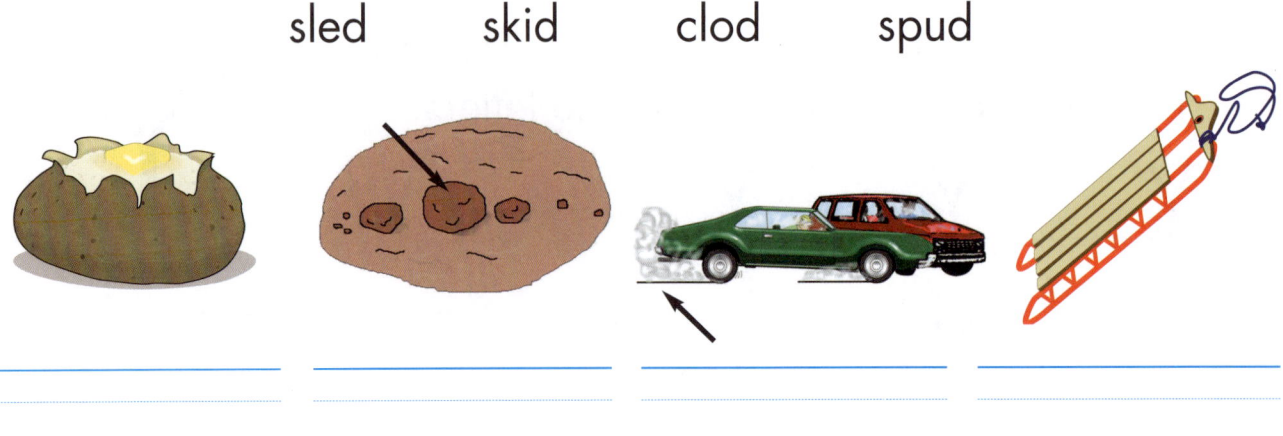

_____   _____   _____   _____

_____   _____   _____   _____

4 Read each word and then write it.

grid _____   plod _____

slid _____   prod _____

   trod _____

                              stud _____

Review These Rules:

Rule 13: If a word has one vowel, the vowel is usually short.
Rule 47: **sk** walks with **e**, **i**, or **y** to make the **sk** sound.

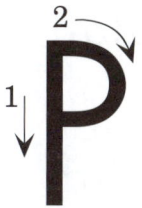
1 Notice how the capital letter **P** is formed. Practice tracing and writing the letters.

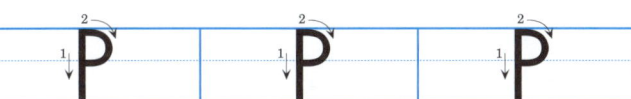

P P P P P P P

P

p

2 Read each word and then write it.

Rule 6
sniff

Rule 6
stiff

Rules 46, 6
sc<u>o</u>ff

Rule 6
bluff

Rule 6
fluff

Rule 6
gruff

Rule 6
stuff

3 Draw a line from the word to the correct picture.

Rule 6
staff

Rule 6
cliff

Rule 46
sc̲uff

4 Read each word and then write it under the correct picture.

Rule 21   Rule 21   Rule 21
drag̅   **flag̅**   **twig̅**

_____ _____ _____

_____ _____ _____

5 Read each word and then write it.

Rule 21
brag̅ _____

Rule 21
stag̅ _____

Rule 21
snag̅ _____

Rule 21
swag̅ _____

Review These Rules:

Rule 6:   If a short-vowel word ends in **f**, **l**, **s**, or **z**, we usually double the final consonant.

Rule 13: If a word has one vowel, the vowel is usually short.

Rule 21: **g** has the hard **g̅** sound at the end of a word.

Rule 46: **sc̲** walks with **a**, **o**, or **u** to make the **sk** sound.

① Notice how the capital letter **Q** is formed.
Practice tracing and writing the letters.

Q   Q   Q

Q   Q   Q   Q   Q   Q

Q

q

② Read each word and then write it.

Rule 21
floḡ _____

Rule 21
smoḡ _____

Rule 21
druḡ _____

Rule 21
sluḡ _____

Rule 21
smuḡ _____

Rule 21
snuḡ _____

③ Read each word and then write it under the correct picture.

Rule 21
cloḡ

Rule 21
froḡ

Rule 21
pluḡ

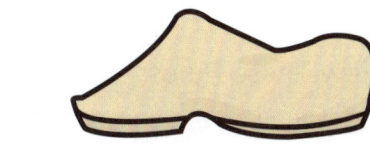

4 Read each word and then write it.

Rule 7
dredge _____

Rule 7
grudge _____

Rule 7
fledge _____

Rule 7
trudge _____

Rule 7
sledge _____

5 Draw a line from the word to the correct picture.

Rule 7
pledge

Rule 7
bridge

Rule 7
smudge

Review These Rules:

Rule 7: In a short word, use dge if the j sound comes right after a short vowel.

Rule 13: If a word has one vowel, the vowel is usually short.

Rule 21: g has the hard ḡ sound at the end of a word.

1 Notice how the capital letter **K** is formed.
Practice tracing and writing the letters.

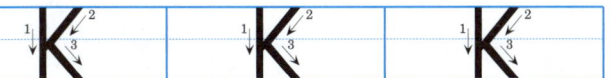

2 Read each word and then write it.

Rule 6
dwell

Rule 6
smell

Rule 6
spell

Rule 6
swell

Rule 6
drill

Rule 6
frill

Rules 47, 6
skill

Rule 6
still

© Mile-Hi Publishers. Do not reproduce.

③ Read each word and then write it under the correct picture.

Rule 6 **grill** Rule 6 **spill** **clam** **slam**

_____   _____   _____   _____

- - - - - - - - -   - - - - - - - - -   - - - - - - - - -   - - - - - - - - -

_____   _____   _____   _____

④ Read each word and then write it.

Rule 6 **trill** _____ **cram** _____

Rule 6 **twill** _____ **swam** _____

Review These Rules:

Rule 6:   If a short-vowel word ends in **f**, **l**, **s**, or **z**, we usually double the final consonant.

Rule 13:   If a word has one vowel, the vowel is usually short.

Rule 47:   **sk** walks with **e**, **i**, or **y** to make the **sk** sound.

1 Practice writing the letters.

A					

a					

2 Draw a line from the word to the correct picture.

stem

brim

slim

3 Read each word and then write it.

grim _____   trim _____

prim _____

Rule 47

skim _____

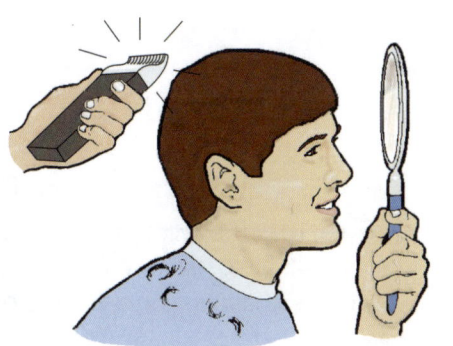

④ Read each word and then write it under the correct picture.

swim　　　drum　　　plum

_____　_____　_____
. . . .　. . . . .　. . . . .
_____　_____　_____

⑤ Read each word and then write it.

from   _____

glum   _____

Rule 46
s<u>c</u>um   _____

slum   _____

swum   _____

Review These Rules:
Rule 13: If a word has one vowel, the vowel is usually short.
Rule 46: **s<u>c</u>** walks with **a**, **o**, or **u** to make the **sk** sound.
Rule 47: **sk** walks with **e**, **i**, or **y** to make the **sk** sound.

1 Practice writing the letters.

B					

b					

2 Read each word and then write it.

bran _____

clan _____

plan _____

Rule 46
s<u>c</u>an _____

span _____

spin _____

spun _____

stun _____

3 Read each word and then write it beside the correct picture.

Rule 47
grin   skin   twin

_____

_____

_____

_____

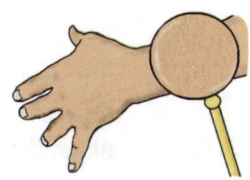

4 Read each word and then write it.

Rule 39
blanch _____

Rule 39
flinch _____

Rule 39
clench _____

Rule 39
brunch _____

Rule 39
stench _____

Rule 39
crunch _____

5 Read each word and then write it under the correct picture.

Rule 39
branch

Rule 39
drench

Rule 39
trench

_____

_____

_____

6 Choose the correct word to finish each sentence and write it on the line.

branch / trench

1. Dad dug a _____ .

branch / trench

2. A _____ hit the shed.

Review These Rules:

Rule 13: If a word has one vowel, the vowel is usually short.

Rule 39: If consonant **l**, **n**, or **r** comes between the vowel and the **ch** sound, it is spelled **ch**.

Rule 46: **sc** walks with **a**, **o**, or **u** to make the **sk** sound.

Rule 47: **sk** walks with **e**, **i**, or **y** to make the **sk** sound.

1 Practice writing the letters.

C

c

2 Read each word and then write it.

clang	clung
sprang	flung
twang	slung
bring	stung
cling	swung
fling	
sting	

3 Read each word and then write it under the correct picture.

_____   _____   _____

4 Choose the correct word to finish each sentence and write it on the line.

clung / flung

1. The tot _____ to his dad.

spring / sprang

2. A cat _____ at the rat.

spring / sting

3. Ben has a _____ in his box.

sling / sting

4. Will this _____ his leg?

Review This Rule:

Rule 13: If a word has one vowel, the vowel is usually short.

1 Practice writing the letters.

D

d

2 Read each word and then write it.

blank _____

clank _____

crank _____

drank _____

frank _____

prank _____

spank _____

stank _____

3 Read each word and then write it under the correct picture.

plank   blink   stink   trunk

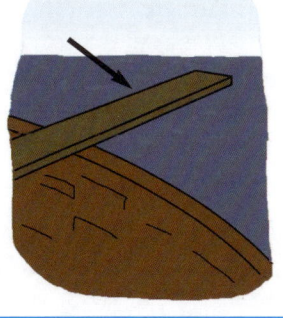   

_____ _____ _____ _____

4 Read each word and then write it.

clink _____   slunk _____

slink _____   spunk _____

drunk _____   stunk _____

5 Choose the correct word to finish each sentence and write it on the line.

trunk / spunk

1. Put this _____ in the shed.

slink / drink

2. When did Frank _____ his milk?

Review This Rule:

Rule 13:   If a word has one vowel, the vowel is usually short.

Name _____

spe

① Practice writing the letters.

E					

e					

② Read each word and then write it beside the correct picture.

clap   snap   trap   flip   trip   stop

_____

_____

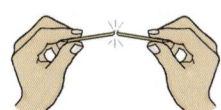

_____

_____

_____

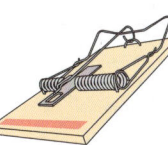

_____

③ Read each word and then write it.

flap   _____

slap   _____

step   _____

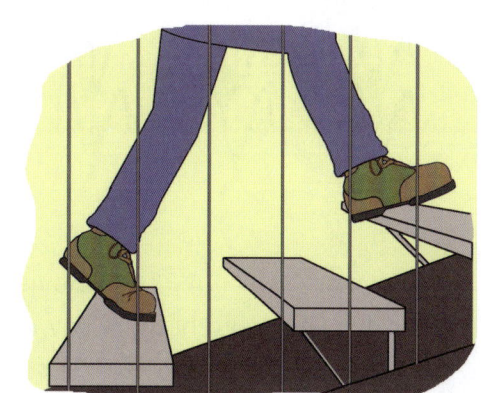

4 Read each word and then write it under the correct picture.

Rule 47

drip   grip   skip   slip

_____   _____   _____   _____

5 Read each word and then write it.

clip   _____   drop   _____

snip   _____   flop   _____

strip   _____   prop   _____

crop   _____   slop   _____

Review These Rules:

Rule 13:   If a word has one vowel, the vowel is usually short.

Rule 47:   **sk** walks with **e**, **i**, or **y** to make the **sk** sound.

Name _____

1 Practice writing the letters.

F					

f					

2 Read each word and then write it.

clash _____

flash _____

slash _____

smash _____

stash _____

flesh _____

fresh _____

swish _____

3 Draw a line from the word to the correct picture.

crash

trash

④ Read each word and then write it.

slush _____   crush _____

blush _____   flush _____

⑤ Read each word and then write it under the correct picture.

brush   slosh

_____

_____

⑥ Choose the correct word to finish each sentence and write it on the line.

slush / swish

1. Six lads ran in the _____.

flush / trash

2. Dad put the _____ in a big can.

crush / blush

3. Did Glen _____ this egg?

Review This Rule:

Rule 13: If a word has one vowel, the vowel is usually short.

Name

1 Practice writing the letters.

G

g

2 Read each word and then write it.

Rule 6
brass

Rule 6
class

Rule 6
bless

Rule 6
press

Rule 6
bliss

Rule 6
gloss

3 Read each word and then write it beside the correct picture.

Rule 6
glass

Rule 6
grass

Rule 6
dress

Rule 6
cross

Rule 6
floss

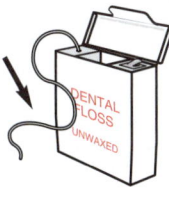

4 Read each word and then write it.

brat _____   spat _____

Rule 46
s<u>c</u>at _____   fret _____

slat _____

5 Look at the picture. Then read the sentence and write it on the line.

Is it flat?

_____

_____

Review These Rules:

Rule 6: If a short-vowel word ends in **f, l, s,** or **z,** we usually double the final consonant.

Rule 13: If a word has one vowel, the vowel is usually short.

Rule 46: **s<u>c</u>** walks with **a, o,** or **u** to make the **sk** sound.

Name

1 Practice writing the letters.

H					

h					

2 Read each word and then write it.

flit _____

grit _____

Rule 47
skit _____

slit _____

spit _____

clot _____

plot _____

slot _____

spot _____

smut _____

3 Choose the correct word to finish each sentence and write it on the line.

skit / slit

1. Josh cut a _____ in his cuff.

fret / skit

2. Rex will not _____ .

4 Read each word and then write it beside the correct picture.

blot   trot

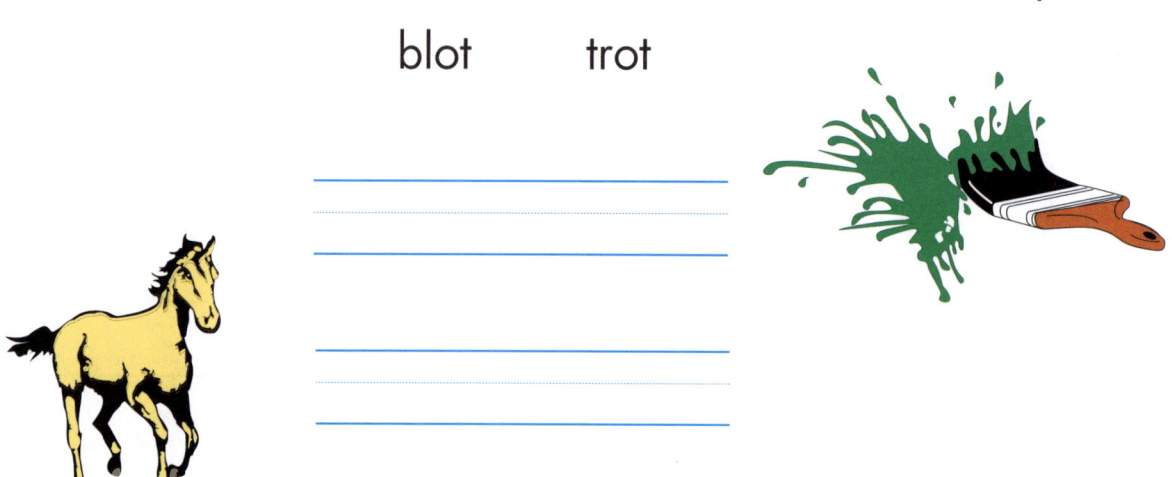

_____

_____

_____

5 Choose the correct word to finish each sentence and write it on the line.

slot / plot

1. Chip will tell us the _____ .

slot / clot

2. Did it fit in that _____ ?

blot / trot

3. Will Brad _____ the ink?

spot / trot

4. Can the nag _____ ?

Review These Rules:

Rule 13:   If a word has one vowel, the vowel is usually short.
Rule 47:   **sk** walks with **e**, **i**, or **y** to make the **sk** sound.

1 Practice writing the letters.

	I					

	i					

2 Read each word and then write it. Note three consonants at the beginning of each word.

Rule 6

thrill _____   strength _____

throb _____   string _____

split _____   strung _____

splint _____   strap _____

3 Read each word and then write it under the correct picture.

thrush   splash   strong

_____   _____   _____

4 Read each word and then write it.

scrap   _____ | shred   _____

Rule 21   _____ | Rule 6   _____
sprig | shrill

   _____ | Rule 21   _____
sprung | shrug

5 Draw a line from the word to the correct picture.

scrub

spring

shrub

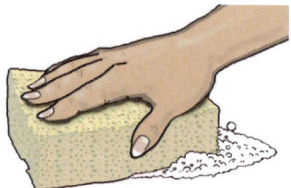

Review These Rules:

Rule 6: If a short-vowel word ends in **f**, **l**, **s**, or **z**, we usually double the final consonant.

Rule 13: If a word has one vowel, the vowel is usually short.

Rule 21: **g** has the hard **ḡ** sound at the end of a word.

1 Practice writing the letters.

J					

j					

2 Draw a line from the word to the correct picture.

Rule 38
scratch

Rule 38
thatch

Rules 47, 38
sketch

Rule 38
switch

Rule 38
crutch

3 Look at the picture. Circle the correct word for the picture and then write it beside the picture.

broth

cloth

froth

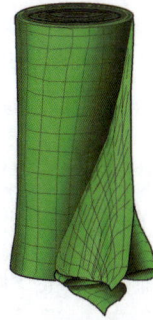

_____

4 Read each word and then write it.

Rule 38
snatch _____

Rule 38
snitch _____

Rule 38
stretch _____

Rule 38
stitch _____

5 Read each word and then write it under the correct picture.

Rule 27
flax

Rule 27
flex

Rule 6
frizz

_____   _____   _____

6 Read each word and then write it.

Rule 38
twitch _____

Rule 38
clutch _____

Rule 38
blotch _____

smith _____

Rule 38
crotch _____

broth _____

Rule 38
splotch _____

froth _____

Review These Rules:

Rule 6:   If a short-vowel word ends in **f**, **l**, **s**, or **z**, we usually double the final consonant.

Rule 13: If a word has one vowel, the vowel is usually short.

Rule 27: Usually **x** at the end of a word has the soft **x** sound.

Rule 38: In a short word, use **tch** if the **ch** sound comes right after a short vowel.

Rule 47: **sk** walks with **e**, **i**, or **y** to make the **sk** sound.

1 Practice writing the letters.

K

k

2 Read each word and then write it.

act

fact

tact

strict

draft

haft

cleft

left

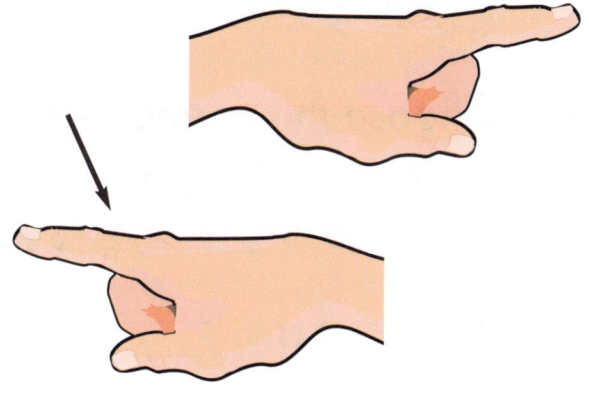

3 Draw a line from the word to the correct picture.

tract

craft

raft

shaft

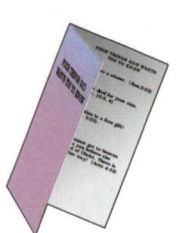

theft

4 Choose the correct word to finish each sentence and write it on the line.

fact / tact

1. Is that a _____ ?

act / fact

2. He did his _____ in the swing.

Review This Rule:

Rule 13: If a word has one vowel, the vowel is usually short.

1 Practice writing the letters.

2 Read each word and then write it.

drift		swift	
shift		thrift	
sift		soft	

3 Read each word and then write it under the correct picture.

lift   loft   bulb   weld

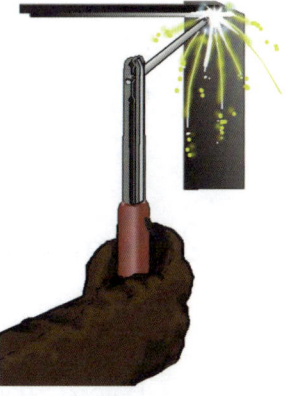

④ Read each word and then write it.

held _____

Rule 4
bulge _____

elf _____

silk _____

self _____

bulk _____

Rule 2
gulf _____

sulk _____

⑤ Read each word and then write it beside the correct picture.

Rule 2
shelf   golf   elk   milk

_____

_____

_____

_____

⑥ Choose the correct word to finish each sentence and write it on the line.

lift / sift

1. Can Kim _____ a big log?

weld / held

2. Tom will _____ the lid.

Review These Rules:

Rule 2:   **g** walks with **a**, **o**, or **u** to make the hard **ḡ** sound.
Rule 4:   **g** walks with **e**, **i**, or **y** to make the soft **g̣** sound.
Rule 13: If a word has one vowel, the vowel is usually short.

1 Practice writing the letters.

M

m

2 Read each word and then write it.

film

help

yelp

Rule 2

ḡulp

pulp

Rule 84

else

3 Read each word and then write it under the correct picture.

Rule 46

elm   scalp   belt   melt

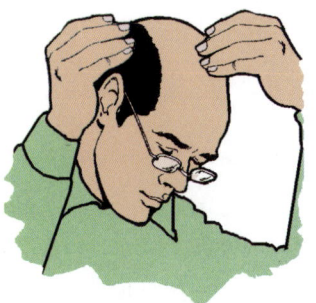

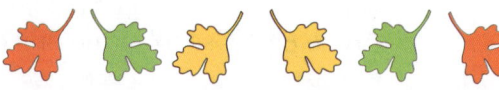

4 Read each word and then write it.

shalt _____

felt _____

welt _____

Rule 5

kilt _____

tilt _____

Rule 85

solve _____

5 Draw a line from the word to the correct picture.

stilt

wilt

Rule 85
valve

Rule 85
twelve

12

Review These Rules:

Rule 2: **g** walks with **a**, **o**, or **u** to make the hard $\bar{g}$ sound.
Rule 5: **k** walks with **e**, **i**, or **y** to make the **k** sound.
Rule 13: If a word has one vowel, the vowel is usually short.
Rule 46: **sc** walks with **a**, **o**, or **u** to make the **sk** sound.
Rule 84: Sometimes a word ends in **se** to make the **s** sound.
Rule 85: Use **ve** at the end of a word for the **v** sound.

1 Practice writing the letters.

N					

n					

2 Read each word and then write it.

Rule 1

c̲amp _____

champ _____

cramp _____

damp _____

Rule 46

sc̲amp _____

tamp _____

tramp _____

3 Draw a line from the word to the correct picture.

clamp

lamp

ramp

4 Read each word and then write it.

hemp _____

Rule 47

skimp _____

crimp _____

pomp _____

limp _____

romp _____

primp _____

5 Read each word and then write it under the correct picture.

stamp   blimp   shrimp

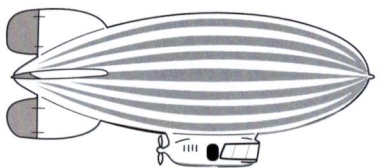

_____

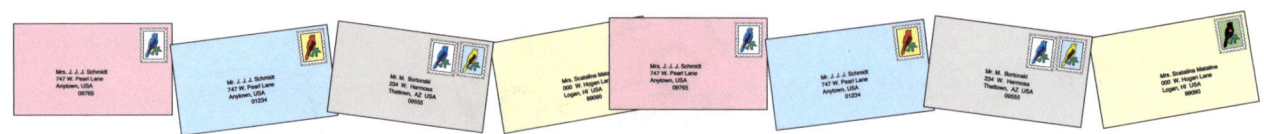

Review These Rules:

Rule 1:   c walks with **a**, **o**, or **u** to make the hard <u>c</u> sound.
Rule 13: If a word has one vowel, the vowel is usually short.
Rule 46: **s<u>c</u>** walks with **a**, **o**, or **u** to make the **sk** sound.
Rule 47: **sk** walks with **e**, **i**, or **y** to make the **sk** sound.

1 Practice writing the letters.

O					

o					

2 Read each word and then write it.

plump _____

slump _____

thump _____

Rule 84

glimpse _____

tempt _____

prompt _____

3 Read each sentence and then write it on the line.

1. Mom put a plump hen in the pot.

_____

2. Beth got a glimpse of the sun.

_____

(4) Circle the correct word for the picture and then write it.

bump
dump
plump
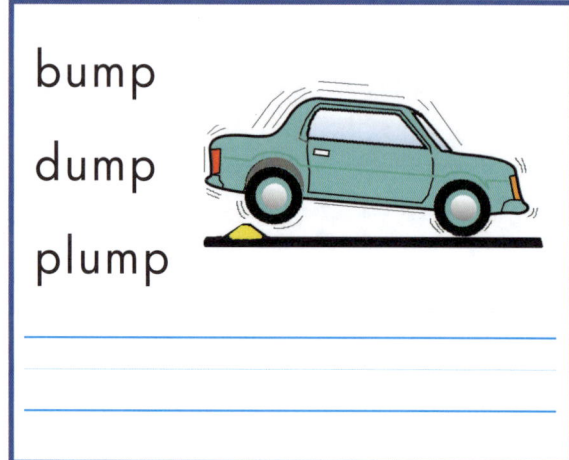
_____

hump
jump
slump

_____

lump
thump
pump
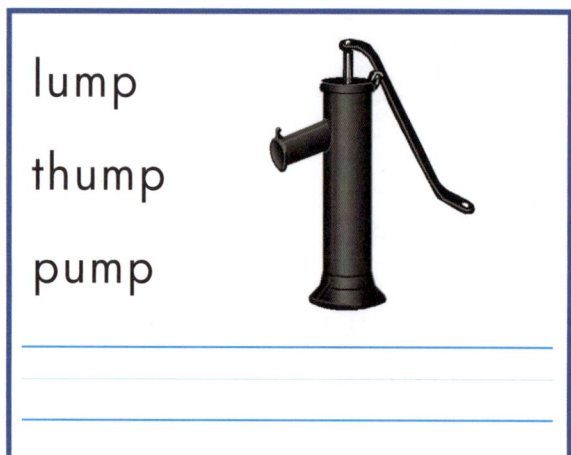
_____

slump
stump
clump

_____

(5) Read each word and then write it.

clump _____

hump _____

dump _____

lump _____

1 Practice writing the letters.

P					

p					

2 Read each word and then write it.

Rule 3
chance _____

Rule 3
dance _____

Rule 3
glance _____

Rule 3
prance _____

Rule 3
fence _____

Rule 3
mince _____

Rule 3
prince _____

Rule 3
since _____

Rule 3
dunce _____

3 Choose the correct words to finish the sentence and write them on the lines.

fence / prince   fence / prince

Did a _____ jump a _____ ?

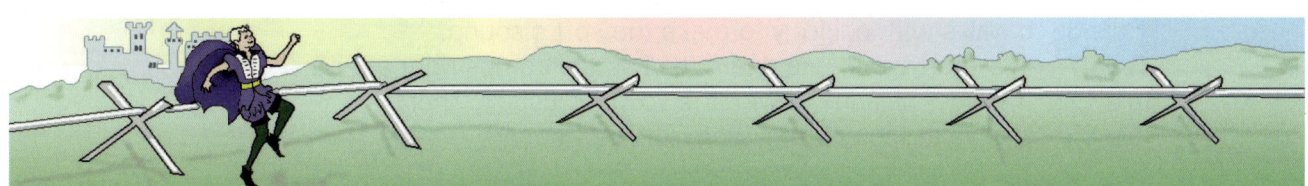

④ Circle the correct word for the picture and then write it.

clip
flip
nip
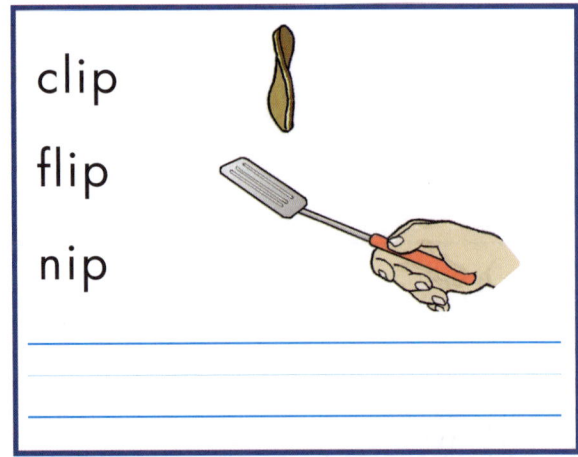
_____

drop
crop
shop
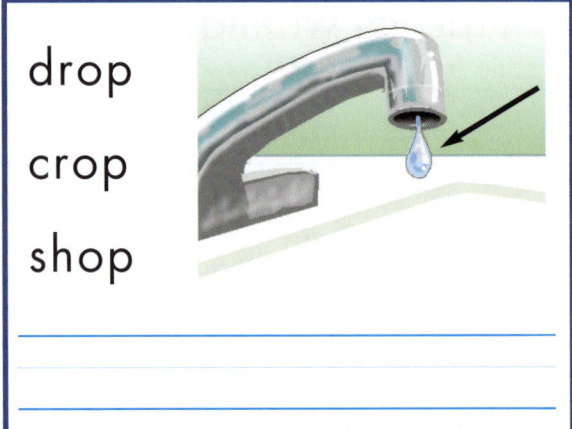
_____

Rule 7
fudge
Rule 7
smudge
Rule 7
judge

_____

help
Rule 2
gulp
yelp
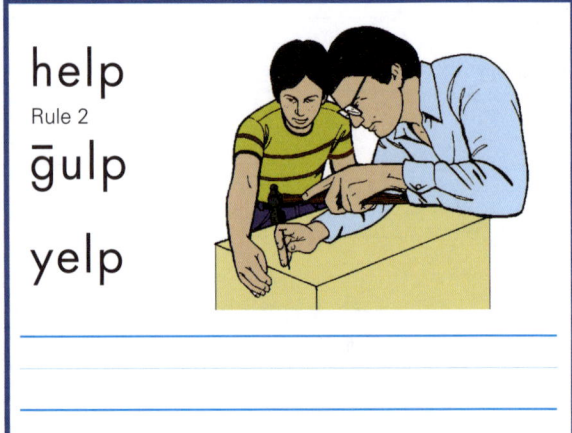
_____

scrub
shrub
stub

_____

Rule 85
solve
Rule 85
valve
Rule 85
twelve

_____

Review These Rules:

Rule 2: g walks with a, o, or u to make the hard g̅ sound.

Rule 3: c walks with e, i, or y to make the soft ç sound.

Rule 7: In a short word, use dge if the j sound comes right after a short vowel.

Rule 13: If a word has one vowel, the vowel is usually short.

Rule 85: Use ve at the end of a word for the v sound.

① Practice writing the letters.

Q

q

② Read each word and then write it under the correct picture.

band   brand   hand   stand

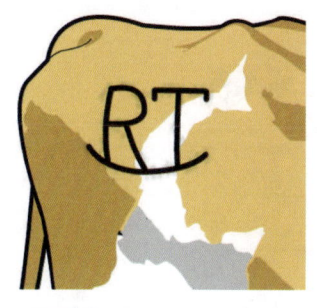   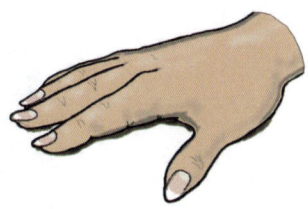      

_____   _____   _____   _____

③ Read each word and then write it.

and _____   bend _____

grand _____   blend _____

land _____   end _____

sand _____   lend _____

4 Read each word and then write it.

mend _____   tend _____

send _____   fond _____

5 Draw a line from the word to the correct picture.

spend

wind

blond

pond

6 Choose the correct word to finish each sentence and write it on the line.

mend / blend

1. Mom will _____ the pink dress.

bend / spend

2. Will Stan _____ his cash?

Review This Rule:

Rule 13: If a word has one vowel, the vowel is usually short.

1 Practice writing the letters.

R

r

2 Circle the correct word for each picture and then write it.

Rule 4
cringe

Rule 4
fringe

Rule 4
hinge

Rule 4
tinge

Rule 4
lunge

Rule 4
plunge

3 Read each word and then write it.

Rule 4
cringe

Rule 4
fringe

Rule 4
tinge

Rule 4
twinge

Rule 4
plunge

4 Draw a line from the word to the correct picture.

rins~~e~~

ant

pants

plant

5 Read each word and then write it.

Rule 84
dens~~e~~ _____

Rule 84
sens~~e~~ _____

Rule 84
tens~~e~~ _____

chant _____

grant _____

pant _____

slant _____

Review These Rules:
Rule 4: **g** walks with **e**, **i**, or **y** to make the soft **ġ** sound.
Rule 13: If a word has one vowel, the vowel is usually short.
Rule 84: Sometimes a word ends in **s~~e~~** to make the **s** sound.

1 Practice writing the letters.

S

s

2 Read each word and then write it.

rent

sent

spent

went

flint

hint

lint

sprint

3 Read each word and then write it under the correct picture.

bent   dent   tent   mint

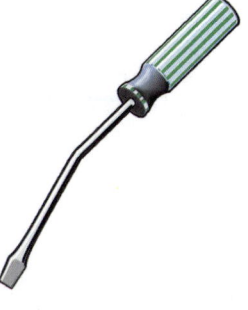

4 Read each word and then write it.

blunt _____   runt _____

grunt _____   stunt _____

5 Circle the correct word for each picture and then write it.

lint
mint
print
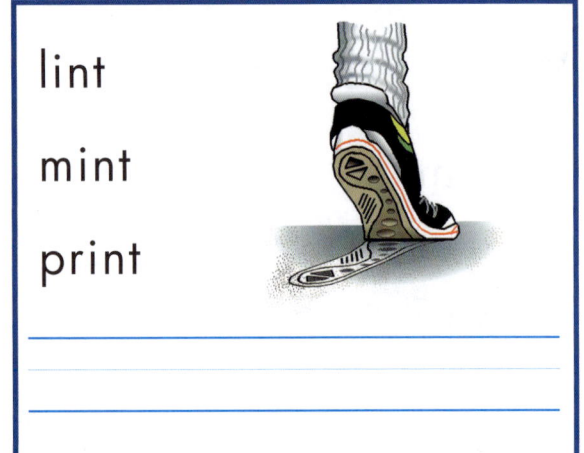
_____

hint
splint
print
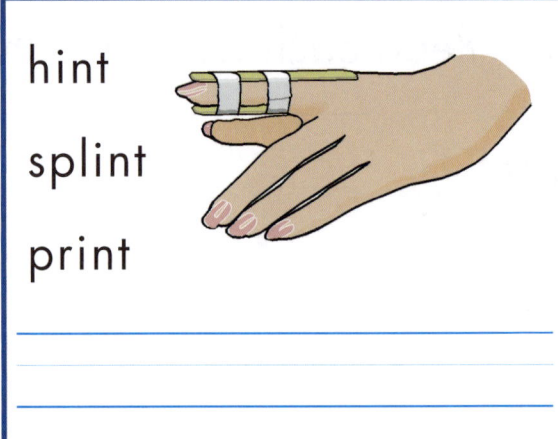
_____

hunt
runt
blunt

_____

grunt
stunt
punt
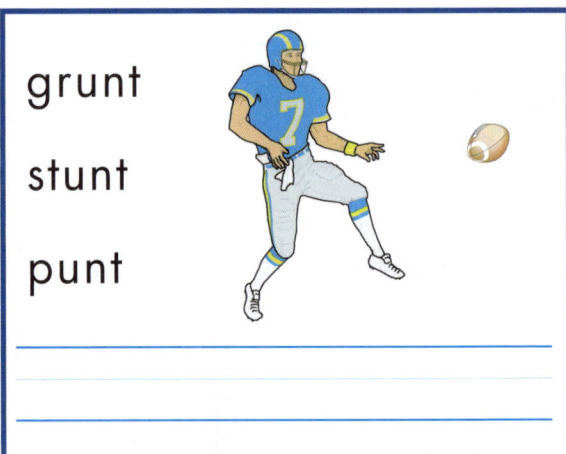
_____

Review This Rule:

Rule 13:   If a word has one vowel, the vowel is usually short.

1 Practice writing the letters.

T

t

2 Read each word and then write it.

Rule 84

lapse

crept

Rule 5

kept

swept

3 Draw a line from the word to the correct picture.

slept

wept

mask

desk

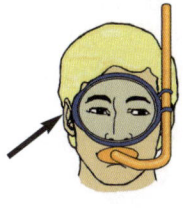

4 Read each word and then write it.

ask _____

bask _____

Rule 1
<u>c</u>ask _____

task _____

brisk _____

risk _____

Rule 37
whisk _____

5 Read each word and then write it beside the correct picture.

flask   disk   husk   tusk

_____   _____

_____   _____

Review These Rules:

Rule 1: **c** walks with **a**, **o**, or **u** to make the hard <u>c</u> sound.

Rule 5: **k** walks with **e**, **i**, or **y** to make the **k** sound.

Rule 13: If a word has one vowel, the vowel is usually short.

Rule 37: Sometimes when **w** and **h** go walking, they make the consonant-digraph sound — **wh**.

Rule 84: Sometimes a word ends in **s̸** to make the **s** sound.

Name _____

1 Practice writing the letters.

U					

u					

2 Read each word and then write it.

Rule 2

ḡasp _____   past _____

crisp _____   vast _____

fast _____   best _____

3 Read each word and then write it beside the correct picture.

Rule 1

clasp   grasp   blast   ͜cast

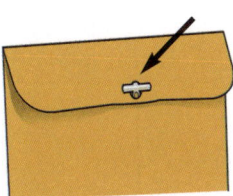 _____

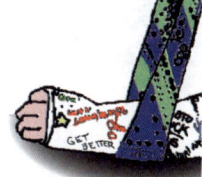 _____

 _____

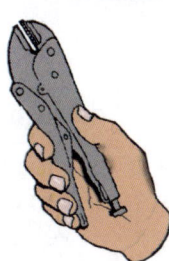 _____

④ Read each word and then write it.

crest _____   rest _____

jest _____   test _____

pest _____   west _____

⑤ Draw a line from the word to the correct picture.

last

chest

nest

vest

Review These Rules:

Rule 1: **c** walks with **a**, **o**, or **u** to make the hard <u>c</u> sound.

Rule 2: **g** walks with **a**, **o**, or **u** to make the hard <u>g̅</u> sound.

Rule 13: If a word has one vowel, the vowel is usually short.

1 Practice writing the letters.

V					

v					

2 Circle the correct word for each picture and then write it.

fist
list
twist

dust
Rule 2
g̅ust
just

crust
just
trust

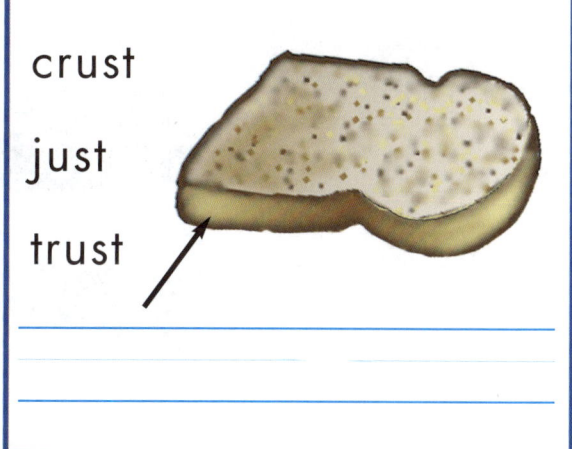

must
thrust
rust

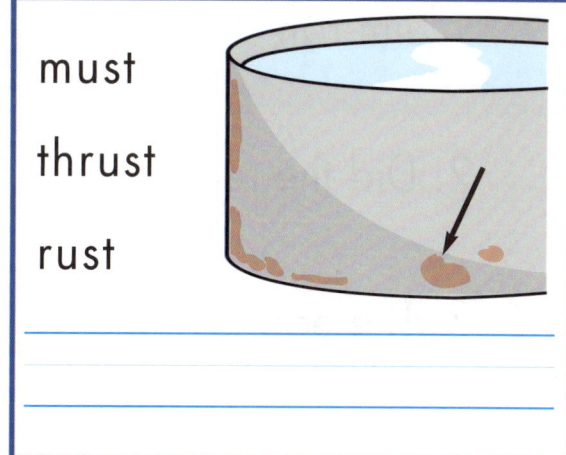

3 Read each word and then write it.

list _____   just _____

twist _____   must _____

Rule 1
c̲ost _____   thrust _____

frost _____   trust _____

lost _____   next _____

dust _____   text _____

4 Choose the correct word to finish each sentence and write it on the line.

fast / fist

1. Jim ran _____ .

dust / rust

2. Did the red van _____ ?

nest / next

3. The egg is in the _____ .

Review These Rules:

Rule 1: c walks with **a**, **o**, or **u** to make the hard c̲ sound.
Rule 2: g walks with **a**, **o**, or **u** to make the hard g̅ sound.
Rule 13: If a word has one vowel, the vowel is usually short.

1 Practice writing the letters.

W

W

2 Read each word and then write it under the correct picture.

| Rule 54 | Rule 54 | Rule 54 | Rule 54 |
| ba¢k | cra¢k | pa¢k | sha¢k |

 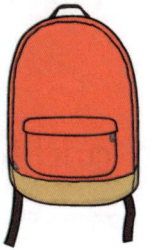 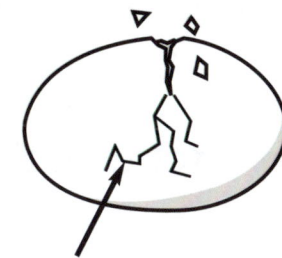

3 Read each word and then write it.

Rule 54
bla¢k

Rule 54
snä¢k

Rule 54
ra¢k

Rule 54
sta¢k

Rule 54
sa¢k

Rule 54
ta¢k

Rule 54
sma¢k

4 Read each word and then write it beside the correct picture.

Rule 54   tra¢k   Rule 54   che¢k   Rule 54   ne¢k   Rule 54   bri¢k   Rule 54   chi¢k   Rule 54   pi¢k

5 Read each word and then write it.

Rule 54   de¢k

Rule 54   pe¢k

Rule 54   spe¢k

Rule 54   cli¢k

Rules 5, 54   ki¢k

Rule 54   li¢k

Review These Rules:

Rule 5:   **k** walks with **e**, **i**, or **y** to make the **k** sound.

Rule 13:   If a word has one vowel, the vowel is usually short.

Rule 54:   In consonant speaker **ck**, **¢** is usually silent and **k** speaks.

Name _____

1 Practice writing the letters.

X					

X					

2 Write the correct word beside each picture. Then write the rest of the words on the lines.

Rule 54	Rule 54	Rule 54	Rule 54	Rule 54
si¢k	sti¢k	thi¢k	ti¢k	tri¢k

 _____

 _____

_____   _____

3 Read each word and then write it.

Rule 54
blo¢k _____

Rule 54
mo¢k _____

Rule 54
flo¢k _____

Rule 54
sho¢k _____

4 Read each word and then write it under the correct picture.

Rule 54
clo¢k

Rule 54
lo¢k

Rule 54
ro¢k

Rule 54
so¢k

_____

_____

_____

_____

5 Read each word and then write it.

Rule 54
clu¢k

_____
_____

Rule 54
stru¢k

_____
_____

Rule 54
lu¢k

_____
_____

Rule 54
stu¢k

_____
_____

Rule 54
plu¢k

_____
_____

Rule 54
tru¢k

_____
_____

6 Choose the correct word to finish each sentence and write it on the line.

duck / cluck

1. Is the _____ stuck?

pluck / truck

2. Is the _____ stuck?

Review These Rules:

Rule 13:   If a word has one vowel, the vowel is usually short.
Rule 54:   In consonant speaker **ck**, ¢ is usually silent and **k** speaks.

Name _____

1 Practice writing the letters.

Y

y

2 Write the correct word beside each picture. Put a slash through each silent letter.

Rule 53	Rule 58	Rule 60	Rule 60	Rules 60, 54	Rule 60
de~~b~~t	~~g~~nat	~~k~~nit	~~k~~nob	~~k~~no~~c~~k	~~k~~not

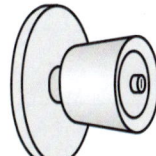 _____

 _____

 _____

 _____

 _____

 _____

3 Choose the correct word to finish the sentence and write it on the line.

knit / knot

Will Fran _____ a tan dress?

4 Draw a line from the word to the correct picture.

Rule 61
lamb

Rule 61
limb

Rule 61
bomb

Rule 61
thumb

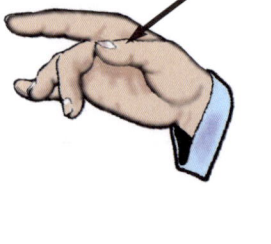

5 Read each word and then write it.

Rule 61
crumb _____

Rule 61
dumb _____

Rule 61
numb _____

Rule 62
hymn _____

Rule 66
scent _____

Review These Rules:

Rule 13: If a word has one vowel, the vowel is usually short.

Rule 53: In consonant speaker **bt**, **b** is silent and **t** speaks.

Rule 54: In consonant speaker **ck**, **c** is silent and **k** speaks.

Rule 58: In consonant speaker **gn**, **g** is silent and **n** speaks.

Rule 60: In consonant speaker **kn**, **k** is silent and **n** speaks.

Rule 61: In consonant speaker **mb**, **m** speaks and **b** is silent.

Rule 62: In consonant speaker **mn**, **m** speaks and **n** is silent.

Rule 66: In consonant speaker **sc** before **e**, **i**, or **y**, **s** speaks and **c** is silent.

1 Practice writing the letters.

Z

z

2 Write the correct word beside each picture.

Rule 69	Rules 69, 54	Rule 69	Rules 69, 39	Rule 69	Rule 69
wrap	wreck	wren	wrench	wrist	wrong

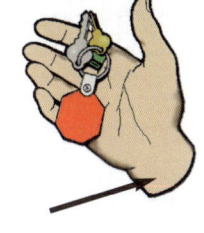

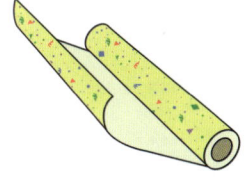

$$\begin{array}{r} 2 \\ +\,2 \\ \hline 5 \checkmark \end{array}$$

3 Draw a line from the word to the correct picture.

Rules 76, 27

phlox

Rule 76

graph

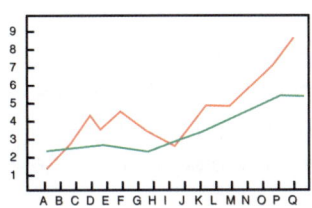

4 Read each word and then write it under the correct picture.

Rules 77, 6   Rule 77   Rules 77, 3   Rule 77

quill   **quilt**   **quince**   **squid**

   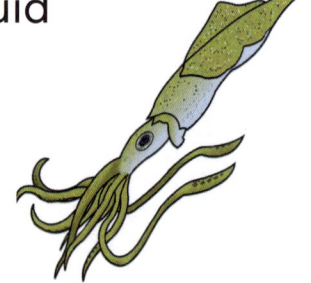

_____   _____   _____   _____

5 Read each word and then write it.

Rules 77, 54
quack _____

Rule 77
quiz _____

Rules 77, 39
quench _____

Rules 77, 39
squelch _____

Rules 77, 54
quick _____

Rule 77
squint _____

Rule 77
quit _____

Rule 77
squish _____

Review These Rules:

Rule 3:   **c** walks with **e**, **i**, or **y** to make the soft **ç** sound.

Rule 6:   If a short-vowel word ends in **f**, **l**, **s**, or **z**, we usually double the final consonant.

Rule 13:   If a word has one vowel, the vowel is usually short.

Rule 27:   Usually **x** at the end of a word has the soft **x** sound.

Rule 39:   If consonant **l**, **n**, or **r** comes between the vowel and the **ch** sound, it is spelled **ch**.

Rule 54:   In consonant speaker **ck**, **c** is usually silent and **k** speaks.

Rule 69:   In consonant speaker **wr**, **w** is silent and **r** speaks.

Rule 76:   Consonant substitute **ph** makes the **f** sound.

Rule 77:   Consonant substitute **qu** or **squ** usually makes the **kw** or **skw** sound.

① Practice writing the letter.

L

It Breaks the Rule!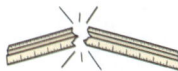

② These words break Rule 6. They do not end in a double consonant. Read each word and then write it on the line.

Rule 40
_th_is _____

Rule 40
_th_us _____

Rule 77
quiz _____

It Breaks the Rule!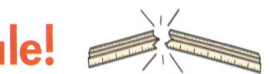

③ This word breaks Rule 4. Usually **g** before **i** has the soft **ġ** sound, but here it has the hard **ḡ** sound. Read the word and then write it on the line.

ḡift _____

It Breaks the Rule!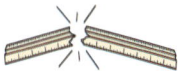

④ This word breaks Rule 47. Usually **sk** before **e**, **i**, or **y** makes the **sk** sound, but here **sk** comes before **u**. Read the word and then write it on the line.

skunk _____

It Breaks the Rule!

5 These words break Rule 38 because **tch** does not follow the short vowel. Read each word and then write it on the line.

rich

much

Rule 37

which

such

Which rich man had so much in such a big bag?

6 These words have the silent letter **l**. Do not forget this letter when you spell and write these words.

Rules 1, 30

c̲al̸f

Rule 30

hal̸f

Review These Rules:

Rule 1: **c** walks with **a**, **o**, or **u** to make the hard c̲ sound.

Rule 4: **g** walks with **e**, **i**, or **y** to make the soft ġ sound.

Rule 6: If a short-vowel word ends in **f**, **l**, **s**, or **z**, we usually double the final consonant.

Rule 30: Note the silent letter in this word.

Rule 37: Sometimes when **w** and **h** go walking, they make the consonant-digraph sound — **wh**.

Rule 38: In a short word, use **tch** if the **ch** sound comes right after a short vowel.

Rule 40: The voiced sound of **th** has a horizontal mark underneath t̲h̲.

Rule 47: **sk** walks with **e**, **i**, or **y** to make the **sk** sound.

Rule 77: Consonant substitute **qu** or **squ** usually makes the **kw** or **skw** sound.

1 Practice writing the letter.

O					

It Breaks the Rule!

2 These words break Rule 13 because they end in **e**, **o**, or **y**. Read each word below and listen to the long-vowel sound. Then write the word on the line.

shē _____

Rule 40
thē _____

frō . _____

prō _____

crȳ _____

drȳ _____

flȳ _____

frȳ _____

plȳ _____

prȳ _____

skȳ _____

slȳ _____

spȳ _____

sprȳ _____

stȳ _____

trȳ _____

shȳ _____

Rule 40
thȳ _____

Rule 37
whȳ _____

3 In these words **o** has the sound of long **ōō**. Listen to your teacher make this sound and then write each word on the line. Also note that the **w** is silent.

Rule 68 _____ Rule 68 _____
who _____ whom _____ two _____

It Breaks the Rule!

4 These words break Rule 13 because the **ȯ** has the sound of short **ŭ**. Read each word and write it, pronouncing **ȯ** with a short **ŭ** sound.

Rule 10 _____ Rule 10 _____
month _____ front _____

5 In these words **ȯ** also has the short **ŭ** sound, but they end in silent **e**. Read each word and write it, pronouncing **ȯ** with a short **ŭ** sound.

Rules 10, 3 * _____ Rules 10, 4 _____
once _____ sponge _____

Review These Rules:

Rule 3:   **c** walks with **e**, **i**, or **y** to make the soft **ç** sound.
Rule 4:   **g** walks with **e**, **i**, or **y** to make the soft **ġ** sound.
Rule 10:   When **o** has the short **u** sound, it is marked **ȯ**.
Rule 13:   If a word has one vowel, the vowel is usually short.
Exception: If a short word with one vowel ends in **e**, **o**, or **y**, the vowel is usually long.
Rule 40:   The voiced sound of **th** has a horizontal mark underneath <u>th</u>.
Rule 68:   In consonant speaker **wh** in a few words, **w** is silent and **h** speaks.
   *   It sounds as if the word **once** begins with **w**, but no **w** is there.

Name

Name

Name